Defining Moments

Angels Among Us

Inspirational Messages From Beyond

Melanie Warner & Amber Torres

To my friend Heather!
Thank you so much for
taking the time to read my
story!
GOD BLESS!

Angels Among Us

Angels Among Us

Praise for *Angels Among Us*

"This book is a great reminder that angels are always around us, if we stay open to the possibility and in tune with that light. Many of the stories made me cry, but also brought me so much joy. Great work!"
- Debra Case

"I would give this book more than 5 stars if I could. The world is full of bad news and dark energy. This book is all about love, light and the true existence of angels, right here with us. The experiences that are shared here are more common than we realize, so it's important to share these stories of hope and inspire others to talk about their own experiences."
- Jason Faulk

"This book brought tears to my eyes. It helped me see how God sends Angels to us all the time. I plan to give this book as a gift of hope to others who are struggling to find light and love in the world"
- Jeff Brown

Angels Among Us

For information about this book or any of our other
Defining Moments ™ books, or to share your own story, - visit:

www.MyDefiningMoments.com
Or Scan the QR Code Below

We are all wishing you so much success in your book journey. Let us
know how we can support you, cheer you on and buy your book!

Melanie Warner
And the Defining Moments Team

Angels Among Us

Dedication

This book is dedicated to my angel, Carson Warner Kennedy, the inspiration behind all of our books and the catalyst for my own transformation.

Melanie Warner

Angels Among Us

Acknowledgments

I want to thank all of the other authors who shared their very personal stories that I hope will inspire you and give you "angel bumps".

I would also like to thank my co-writer and editor, Amber Torres, for her dedication, loyalty, hard work and tireless pursuit of amazing stories.

In addition, I would like to send a special thank you to our Defining Moments team; production manager, Micah Requita and book designer, Jasmin Marcos for their daily commitments and the tightrope of multiple deadlines.

Melanie Warner

Angels Among Us

Table of Contents

Introduction

I have been collecting stories for this book for a few years. I wanted to include stories from people who I personally knew or things that I had witnessed firsthand. Many of the stories that you will read might be hard for some of you to believe.

This is why I curated the specific collection of stories from credible sources over the years. I wanted them to be undeniable and help you have conviction for the existence of angels in our lives.

Most religions believe in angels and souls, even if they disagree with the dogma or interpretation of religious translations or beliefs. This book is not designed to spark a religious debate or encourage you to change your own beliefs, rather a testimony of people who shared their own personal experiences.

You'll find a common theme of angels appearing shortly after prayer. That is also very common in the multiple stories that I have heard about or witnessed during this process. It didn't matter if the person praying was Christian, Jewish, Catholic, Muslim or from another religious background.

You'll read about how some people heard a voice, while others felt a physical presence or touch and still others felt or saw something unexplainable. The goal of this book is to help people who are looking for hope, light or answers about their own encounters.

You'll learn about the different ways that angels interact or engage with us and how common it truly is.

We hope this book blesses you, inspires you and encourages you to be open to having your own angel experience - right here on Earth.

Melanie Warner

CHAPTER 1

THE VOICE OF AN ANGEL

A Special Bond
Melanie Warner

I lived in the Los Angeles area, while the rest of my family lived in Texas. When I had my daughter, Kyla, I was grateful to be able to spend time with my Great Aunt, Victoria Tappan, who was ninety-five years young. She and Kyla quickly formed a strong bond. They were the oldest and youngest living relatives in our family.

One day, we were at Griffith Park in Los Angeles. This was a huge park in a metropolitan area, so there was a road with fast-moving cars and much traffic that went throughout the park. My husband headed to the car and was planning to drive back around and pick us up. He had to cross over the main road to get to our car.

Kyla was next to me, wearing a bright green dress with flowers on it. She was a cute toddler who had just learned how to walk. I turned to help another kid take the wrapper off his ice cream and when I turned back - Kyla had vanished. She was nowhere to be found. I started screaming her name, running around the park and looking everywhere.

Then I saw a small speck of green - far away. I didn't know she had also learned how to run! Kyla was chasing after her Dad who was going to get the car. He had a hearing loss and did not know that Kyla had followed him. He could not hear me yelling for him to turn around.

She was running straight towards the busy street with cars coming around a blind corner at fifty-five miles per hour! I ran as fast as I could, but I knew I could not catch her in time. I was terrified to see what was about to happen, knowing I could not stop it.

Just as she got to the main road and was about to step in front of a car, suddenly she froze, looked up - took a step back and began to cry.

When I finally caught up to her, I asked what had happened to make her stop?

She said in her little toddler voice, "I heard Aunt Vickie say, 'No, Kyla, no' and I couldn't see her and it scared me."

Aunt Vickie had died two weeks earlier. I had not told Kyla about her death as I didn't think she would understand since she was barely walking and talking. Aunt Vickie was also buried in Forest Lawn Cemetery, which was just a few yards from this park.

I believe her voice served as an angel to my daughter and saved her life that day.

Melanie Warner is the founder and publisher of the Defining Moments book series. She loves having a platform to help people share inspiring and uplifting stories. She also helps people write, publish and launch a book. She can be reached at: melanie@mydefiningmoments.com For more info on sharing your story, or writing your own book, visit: www.MyDefiningMoments.com

Scaring Ted Bundy
Laura Duncan

I don't know if anyone else would have heard the voice in 1974. At the time, I was a nineteen-year-old college girl working alone at a Circle K on the evening shift in North Tucson, Arizona. I had agreed to go on a date with a man who had come in the store earlier in the afternoon.

My father had said I would know if a man was good by looking into his eyes, and he had beautiful blue eyes. I agreed to go out with him after I closed out at the end of my shift at 11:00 pm. Looking out the window at closing, I thought it was a little strange that he had parked out by the road instead of up in front of the store, but I was still focused on closing out my shift.

As I was counting money, I heard a woman's voice yell loudly and urgently, "DON'T GO OUT!!!" It was like someone was screaming, only inside my head. But it was as clear as if someone was standing next to me.

It shook me to the core that she sounded so concerned so I locked the door and tried to pretend I wasn't there by sitting low behind the counter until he left.

I took extra care to ride my bike on the back streets just to be sure he didn't find me. Somehow it didn't seem strange to me that I'd heard a woman's voice yell a warning. I'm not sure if I even told my sister what had happened when I arrived home. But two nights later I was at the cash register when he was suddenly standing in front of me.

I said, "Oh I'm sorry I couldn't go out the other night -something came up."

He replied, "Oh I wasn't here anyway."

Now I knew he was a liar and there was no way I was going to go out with him, so I walked him to the door to let him out.

I had already prepared for closing by pulling the sliding door almost shut. We had to face each other as he had to slide through sideways. I had the industrial padlock in my hand to lock it after him. He reached out and grabbed my upper private part with one hand and lower private part with the other. When he grabbed me, I responded with rage, raising my fist over his head with the padlock in it and roared, "GET OUT!!!" I was going to smash his skull open.

I scared him. I saw fear on his face and he stepped outside. I slammed and locked the door, and my legs gave out. The police came quickly, and we went through all the local mug shots, but his face wasn't in there. It was easy to remember what looked like a yellow Volkswagen in the streetlights, but I hadn't been able to read the license plate from so far away.

I remember him saying he'd be back so one of the policemen came after his shift was over for the next few nights. I would like to thank that kind man for making me feel safe.

Over the next decade, I saw stories about the serial killer, Ted Bundy, after he was finally caught and realized that he was the guy! It was too difficult to process and accept. fifteen years later, long after he'd been executed, I happened to see a magazine cover with pictures of ten teenage girls who had been murdered by Bundy. I looked just like them, with long ash blonde hair parted in the middle. So there really was a serial killer waiting for me in that yellow Volkswagen and he didn't even have a seat for me in the car.

I hadn't been ready to face that I had come that close to such a torturous death. Upon seeing the magazine, I began to shake, and I shook for three days. Every time I told my story I would shake for a long while so of course I didn't like talking about it. It has taken all these years to want to share.

I share with the hope that it will help others heed to angelic warnings. I could have easily dismissed the voice and said, "Oh, it will be alright!" I thank God that I listened and didn't go out.

Laura Annette Duncan lives in Clovis, California where she teaches classical piano. Laura is an ordained minister and loves to share her stories and play anointed piano arrangements wherever she is invited. Laura is currently writing a book about life being a test and has many stories of angelic guidance and deliverance. Her album, Keyboards from Heaven, is an hour of sacred melodies with a heavenly sound. Laura enjoys planting things and riding her horse, Penelope. She has two adult daughters, Jessica Christine, and Sarah Lee Rose. You can contact Laura at lauraplayspiano.com

Laura's high school graduation photo (1972)

Slow Down
Amber Torres

It was 2010, I was a college student driving to my internship in downtown Fresno.

The freeway was one floor above ground, it was the kind of freeway entrance that loops around like the bottom of a corkscrew so that you wind up traveling in the direction opposite the one you entered.

It had just started to sprinkle, nothing unusual for this time of year in the central valley. It was an extremely light sprinkle; I could see tiny drops that almost looked like mist on my windshield and some regular drops.

As I ascended the one story (corkscrew style) a voice told me very slowly and clearly, "Slow down....you could get in a car accident." I didn't hear the words audibly but heard them in my mind and felt them in my chest. I knew I was being given a warning.

"Slow down??? I'm going thirty-five miles per hour," I thought to myself but heeded to the instruction.

I released pressure off the gas pedal to decelerate and watched my speedometer go from thirty-five miles per hour to seventeen miles per hour. I was traveling seventeen miles per hour by the time I reached the top of the ramp to merge onto the freeway.

A few moments after I merged onto the right lane of the freeway, my car hydroplaned. It felt like I was gliding on ice as my car spun clockwise not once but twice at a freakishly slow speed. As it was occurring, I actually thought, "I'm going so slow."

When I came to a stop, my car was facing the direction of oncoming traffic but there were no cars. The freeway was completely empty. This was not typical for this time of the morning in my town. I was also close enough to the side of the freeway that I probably would have slid right off the edge and dropped had I been going even just a tiny bit faster. The perfectly clear roadway gave me ample time to turn my car around without the threat of being rammed into by oncoming traffic.

There is no doubt in my mind that I would have either crashed into another car or fell off the freeway had I not listened to the voice. There were cars right by me when the voice told me to slow down. Had I continued driving at the speed I was going when I received the warning I would have most likely crashed into another vehicle when my car hydroplaned because I would have been surrounded by cars. Instead, I slowed down creating distance between my car and the surrounding cars.

I am very grateful that I listened to the voice which I firmly believe was the voice of the Holy Spirit.

"But when the Father sends the Advocate as my representative—that is, the Holy Spirit—he will teach you everything and will remind you of everything I have told you." John 14:26

Amber Torres was born and raised in Central California. She is the mother of Gabriel (23) and Victoria "Vicky" (14). She serves as a volunteer Child Ambassador for World Vision; a Christian Humanitarian organization that works to address the root causes of poverty and injustice (www.worldvision.org). As a soon-to-be empty nester, she looks forward to getting her pilot's license and globe trotting.

Angels Among Us

CHAPTER 2

THE KINDNESS OF STRANGERS

My Own Arch Angel
Maribel Sorensen

I was diagnosed with Stage One pancreatic cancer and had to have a central pancreatectomy surgery to save my life.

"You're lucky we found it early," they said

I said, "It was God!"

I had all the normal fears with this news but, I had a secret weapon: the intercessory prayer of hundreds of people behind me, pleading to my Jesus for a successful surgery and removal of all my cancer!

This is a story about the intersection of heaven and earth in my life and the proof of a loving and real God! I had many people praying for me, "My Prayer Peeps" while I was in the hospital and for months before. I knew in my gut that this would bring God glory!

Join me at my hospital bedside now:

When I woke up in the hospital, I had a NG tube down my throat which went into my stomach. It was very uncomfortable and downright painful. It made it hard to talk and swallow. It kept me awake constantly. I was very weary of all of this and all the rest of my many connections. All I could think about was how hungry I was!

At one point, I was jerked out of my sleep by the sound of me ordering food in my dream.

"Number one...number two..." Yikes!

My fourth day in the hospital landed on a Sunday. I still hadn't had any food and was being nourished by IV fluid.

I decided to watch my church service on my phone. I prayed for the Lord to remove my NG tube and asked my "prayer peeps" to do the same.

I don't recall ringing the bell for a nurse to come so I could ask about getting the NG tube removed and maybe having some real food. I was slightly apprehensive at the thought of the pain of having the tube removed.

A few minutes after 9:00 am, while I was watching my church service, a new nurse entered the room. I had a great nurse but, this was not her. I often had floater nurses care for me, but I had never seen this male nurse. He was just jovial, so happy and had the biggest smile coming in the door. Nothing flashy, but his smile filled with beautiful teeth. I asked him how he was.

He replied, "I'm living the Dream!"

I thought. He must have had some great days off. I just felt that he must be a believer in Jesus. So, I asked him, "You must know your purpose? You know Jesus made you for this job?"

He said, "You bet'cha!"

We made some small talk about God, and he turned to the computer screen and said, "It looks like someone has put in an order to get your tube out."

I said, "You have got to be kidding! I get to eat?"

He said, "Well eventually you will get to eat."

I started to cry from the thought of the pain of having this tube pulled out. The nurse said, "We can take our time."

Usually, floater nurses were in and out quickly. He then said, "Would you like me to pray for you?"

I said, "Yes please."

After he prayed for me, I said, "Go ahead and pull out the tube."

I closed my eyes and in less than two seconds it was out! No pain at all. It was just a little nasty taste. Unbelievable! My nurse was still in the same spot. I had no idea what he did with the tubes because I never saw or heard them be disposed of in the garbage at the foot of my bed.

He said, "You are all done! Have a blessed day!"

He walked out the door and three to five seconds later my regular nurse came in the door just after he left. She stopped short to say, "I see you got your tube out!"

I said, "Yes! That really nice nurse that just left, took it out. His name was Gabriel."

My nurse said. "I don't know what you are talking about."

I said again in a quizzical manner, "You know the African American nurse named Gabriel?"

She just looked at me blankly and said, "Don't know who you are talking about? We don't have a nurse named Gabriel."

I thought, *"Well that was weird."*

Since I had less things hooked up to me, I grabbed my walker as soon as I could and hit my unit floor looking for my nurse Gabriel. No sign or whereabouts anywhere? I looked three times and had no luck.

"Just crazy," I thought. That afternoon my doctor came in and just stared at me reading a book in a chair and said, "Well it looks like you are much better and ready to eat and be discharged." He ordered a meal and I had broth and Jell-O that evening. So great!

I woke up on my first night outside of the hospital in tears at 5:30 am. I realized that God had sent his angel Gabriel to care for me and answer my prayers. I just wept.

I was not any more special to Him than someone else. He was simply demonstrating His love for me. Then, I smiled because I realized... wait... my nurse had no mask on the whole time! And he wore no gloves to take out my tube! All the nurses were required to wear gloves and a mask, no exception. Then I knew 100% that my nurse was an angel!

A few weeks later I got the news that the pancreas tissue removed had tightly close-knit cells only. No spread of cancer and all my lymph nodes came back clean! God would get the glory! My doctor said I was cured and needed nothing else! Thank God!

I am a grateful servant who knows without a shadow of doubt that God hears us. He wants you to know that He loves you and is waiting for you to speak to Him. I am blessed to have had a visit from a guardian angel in the hospital. I believe we entertain angels far more than we realize.

Maribel Sorensen lives in CA. She has been a Christian since she was fifteen years old. In her fifty years of life, she has experienced much pain, tears, and happiness. Without her faith, she doesn't know how she would have coped with all the landmines that have come her way. Her faith has given her a level of peace that transcends all understanding. She credits the Joy of the Lord for changing her mindset in the hardest of times. May this story be evidence that God is searching for you and hears your cries in the darkness. Know that He loves you, He loves you, He loves you!

The Good Samaritans
Matt Epstein

It was 1977 and I was only seven years old when this story took place. This incident happened to my late mother; I will remember it until I have taken my last breath.

One early morning while I was at school and my father was at work, my mother decided to try and hang some drapes in the kitchen while she was home alone. Everything was going to plan as she was measuring and hanging the drapes until she accidently lost her balance while standing on a step ladder. As she fell, her entire elbow went through the window and she began bleeding profusely.

She realized that her main artery was cut and she was losing blood very quickly. Not knowing exactly what to do, she started to panic and grabbed anything she could grab to try and wrap it around her wrist to stop the bleeding. It was not working and at this point, panic had settled in and taken over her mind.

She sat there on the kitchen floor too weak to scream out to anyone for help and too weak to pick up the phone and dial for help. She finally came to surrender thinking of nothing other than my father and I walking into the house only to find her dead on the floor.

It was at this point when, out of nowhere, the front door opened and in walked two men described to look very normal and casually dressed. My mother managed to mutter the question, "Who are you?" One man replied, "That isn't important, the only thing that's important right now is stopping your bleeding and calling an ambulance for you. We also need to call your husband."

At this point, the two men knew exactly the perfect knot to tie to stop the bleeding. Then they proceeded to call the ambulance. After they called the ambulance, they knew exactly what number to dial to reach my father and explained to him what had happened and that they have already called the ambulance and that she will be just fine. When my father asked who they were, the man on the phone simply replied, "Not important, I'm just doing my deed. The only thing important is that you come home and wait with her for the ambulance as we have to leave now and won't be back."

When my mother finally arrived at the hospital, her doctor informed her that these men could not have tied a better knot to stop the bleeding and it saved her life.

The neighbor next door later expressed to the media and to us that he had been in his front yard for over an hour working on his yard and never witnessed anyone coming nor going from our home.

To this day, there has never been closure on who these gentlemen were, but we can only explain it as an act from God. They would not reveal who they were to my mother, nor to my father but we thanked God for them every day. Because of these angels, we were able to have my mother for many more years.

She finally succumbed to cancer in 2006, but thankfully, we had so many years to make and have many wonderful memories.

Matthew Epstein was born in 1970 in Granada Hills, CA and moved to Fresno, CA in 1992. In 2001, he married Tracey Epstein. They still reside in Fresno, CA. Matt can be reached at email: mfe9801@gmail.com

The Key is to Pray
Rick Alonzo

I am a speed painter and martial artist that travels to different churches and venues in various locations to present the gospel in the form of art. I always go to various places as God leads with the goal of inspiring people and bringing them the good news of the gospel of Jesus Christ.

On this particular day I found myself in Wisconsin getting ready to present at a youth service at a local church. Since I had traveled from California, I was staying with members of the congregation who lived about an hour from the church. As I was presented with my luggage and equipment for the event that night, I suddenly realized that I did not have the key for my luggage with me. I had left it at my host's house- an hour away.

I found myself in a major predicament because the event started in an hour. If I were to go to the house to grab the key then return to the church, I would arrive back at the church an hour after the event was scheduled to start…and I would still need ample time to set up.

I was on my knees praying and desperately trying to figure out what to do. *Should I break the lock, or should I send somebody to the house and delay the event for two hours?*

With my eyes closed I began asking God for help. I reminded him that it was Him who opened this door for me to share the gospel with the residents of Wisconsin. "Lord, if you can help me out in this, I sure could use Your help right now"

As soon as I said amen, I opened my eyes. Standing in front of me was a little girl.

She asked me what I was doing. I told her, "I'm trying to get ready for the event and I don't have the key to open my luggage." As these words were coming out of my mouth, I noticed something dangling around her neck. I couldn't believe my eyes…It was a neck chain with one key on it.

I said to her, "Can I borrow the key on your neck chain?"

"Oh, of course, here, you can have it," she said. Then she just ran off.

I quickly used the key to try to open my luggage and it was a perfect fit. Lo and behold it worked …my luggage popped right open.

I got ready that night and did what I had to do. It was a beautiful evening made even more special by the unique set of circumstances that allowed it to transpire.

I will never forget this incident because God was with me all along. In fact, I strongly believe that He is with all of us. We just have to have eyes to see.

I am reminded of the scripture that says, "Ask and you shall receive, seek and you shall find, knock and the door will be opened to you."

I'm not sure who that little girl was. I'd like to think of her as someone whom God sent to help me. She may even be an angel. I didn't see her after that. All I know is that God provided me with what I needed to accomplish my work that night. He knew that I would be in that predicament ahead of time, and He had already prepared a way. He sent me there and He provided everything I needed to accomplish what He sent me to do.

"For I know the plans I have for you," declares the Lord, "plans to prosper you and not to harm you, plans to give you hope and a future." *Jeremiah 29:11*

I thank God for answered prayers.

Rick Alonzo is an evangelist, speaker, artist, and performer. He is the Founder and President of Rick Alonzo Ministries, a nonprofit organization committed to reaching the world and impacting the lives of people. As an ordained minister, his main focus is to proclaim the gospel through art, music, and motion. He lives in California and has been married to his wife Michelle for twenty-seven years. They have three incredible adult children and one awesome teen.

Comfort From a Stranger
Laurraine Kotara

My story begins when my daughter, Danielle, was five years old. She was born with Hydrocephalus, which meant she had water on the brain. As a result of the damage to her brain, she also had Epilepsy.

She had been going to Pre-K and Kindergarten at a Catholic School in Dallas, Texas. I was informed by her teacher that she was not keeping up and that Daneille would have to be taught under Section 504 of the Texas Education Agency. The teacher said this was the case because she was showing to be mentally challenged. I asked her what that meant and she stated that children with mental or intellectual disabilities are protected under this Section. She went on to say that she would not be able to attend the private school and would have to be enrolled in public school because they can accommodate students with intellectual disabilities. I was clearly upset. To make matters worse, the teacher came across as rude and insensitive. This was also upsetting to me. I went to the principal of the school and she sided with the teacher and again explained that they are not able to accommodate students such as Danielle.

I took Danielle to my mother's house. I called Father John, who was in charge of the school finances and told him I wanted a full refund. I started to tell him what happened and began crying. I could barely get through the conversation. He was very compassionate and apologized for my being treated that way. He assured me that I would get a full refund. We did.

After I hung up I cried harder than I think I have ever cried. I was upset about what was going to happen to Danielle. *How she was going to get through life and how she was going to be treated by others? How was I going to handle having a mentally challenged child?* So many things were going through my mind. While I was crying, it suddenly felt like someone put their hand on my shoulder and it was as if God or my Guardian Angel was telling me that everything was going to be okay. I looked around and no one was there, but I felt instantly better.

Later I went to Wal-Mart and I was looking in an aisle with Christmas decorations. I kept seeing an older lady. I went along and ran into her again in another aisle. She asked me if anything was the matter. I don't know why, but I told her the whole story. She said, "All will be fine. I had two children with special needs and they grew up and are going through life just fine."

I thanked her for making me feel better and started to walk away. I quickly turned back around to ask her another question and she was gone. I looked everywhere, as she could not have gone far. It was seconds since I had talked to her. It was as if she disappeared. I believe she was an angel.

Laurraine Kotara is a proud Texas native. Her daughter Danielle is a high functioning special needs adult. Because of the Hydrocephalus she was not expected to live past five years old, but she is now twenty-seven. So maybe the angels are still watching. The Hydrocephalus Association https://www.hydroassoc.org and Epilepsy Foundation https://www.epilepsy.com are good resources for those seeking information on either medical condition.

Angels In the Outfield
By Linda Espinoza

Do you believe in angels, divine intervention, God? I do. I've spent countless moments where it was nothing but the grace of God that could make something happen. This story I share is testament that He places angels in our lives to guide our direction and decisions; angels to protect us, and angels to comfort us in our times of need.

It was 2013. We had had a couple of tough years, mixed with joy. I say mixed, because we had finally come home to the place I'd longed to be all my married life. After living in Mendota for twenty-three years and living in Fresno for nine months, God literally brought our family full circle and back to Firebaugh. It was just enough time to birth a dream that had burned in my heart for so long, I could taste it.

A year after moving to my precious, little town of Firebaugh, my husband, Salami (Salome), was diagnosed with ALS. It would prove to be the greatest challenge of our lives. But in the midst of darkness, there was light. There were, as I like to say, "Angels in the Outfield." Everything from our angels blessing us with a mobility van to transport Salami and his powerchair. Our angel that blessed us with a scooter when Salami could no longer walk on his own. Angels that gifted us with a hoyer lift to save us from the strain of lifting Salami. These were only a few because I could go on about the presence of God through these angels of grace that showed up in our hour of need.

Then there was the one that would change the trajectory of our lives. This Angel made a way for us to buy our home. It was the fall of 2013, I had been walking every morning for my physical and emotional health. Daily, I'd walk on the street we lived on because there was a property I had hoped to build our new home on. Only they weren't selling, but that was okay because I was praying and believing they would. Salami spoke to the owner who confirmed that wasn't going to happen. In an almost shift of fate, I began to feel a pull toward another home on my street. It was as if it was calling me. After one of my walks, I went home and was looking for a paper I needed in my cabinet. Low and behold, I pulled out a flyer with the exact house down the street that seemed to be calling me towards it. It had previously been up for sale, or foreclosure, which is why I had the flyer.

Later that night my nephew Michael, while visiting, asks us if we had heard the house down the street was going to auction. I knew then it was not a coincidence. So, Salami and I strategized on how we would try to buy it. With only three weeks before auction, it was near impossible to get a loan or sell property we had. We did the only thing that came to mind – ask to borrow it. But who on Earth would let us borrow that much money? I know it's insane – but we were willing to be insane for the sake of something I believed with all my heart could be ours. What I didn't say was, we needed this home because of the space that Salami would require for what was about to come through his ALS journey.

On the day I asked to borrow the money from our friend, I prayed. I prayed and had been praying, if it was God's will, our friend would say yes. It was one of the hardest things I've ever done. Only God could've given me this kind of boldness because at this point, I rarely liked to ask for help. Our friend said, "Yes," without hesitation and asked, "when do you need it?" My ears could not believe I heard the word, yes! It was a miracle!! We were beyond grateful for our angel in the outfield!! Beyond grateful that God said yes, first.

Fast forward to auction day, and again another God moment. I believe there were only three bidders in attendance, and no one from

Firebaugh. As they opened up the bidding, we were aware we only had so much money to work with.

The bidding continued… we were almost out of money. Salami said, "That's it, Linda, we can't bid anymore." I said, "No, Fatty… it's our home. I know it!" I took the bidder number from his hand and kept bidding. Finally, it ended, and we won the bid. Only, we were $12,000 short of the seller's bid!! At once the foreclosing bank came to ask us if we had a cashiers check for the remaining balance, as they already had the checks we submitted to open up the bidding. We told them no, but we could go get a cashier's check. They responded with, "I'm sorry but that's not the way it works. You must have it in hand, or we will have to put the house back up for auction."

I felt my heart sink, but I had already told Salami we had a check in the truck, and I could go to the bank to get a cashier's check. Salami, in his broken speech, due to the ALS, asked if we could run to the bank – only God and an angel acting on his behalf could say yes – and he did. He told us they had never done this before, but they'd give us thirty minutes, or it would be on the auction block again. I literally ran to the truck and back, asking on my way if anyone knew where the bank was, and no one knew.

Suddenly, as I was about ready to go, a person I'd like to say was an angel, came and gave me directions. Off I went running in my wedge sandals. Mind you it was September in the Central Valley, and it was hot! I ran for five or six blocks, aware of my thirty-minute time limit, only to get to the end and find nothing. I called Salami and he told me it should be there. I looked to my right and sure enough it was behind a closed building.

I entered, still not sure if I could get the cashier's check, due to only Salami's name being on the check. With only one person in line, I asked for the check and without hesitation, I was given the amount needed. How do you spell RELIEF?! I couldn't stop thanking God. He placed every angel in our path to make this all possible. It was then that I called Salami to let him know that I had the check in hand.

I then ran back, praying and sweating that after being so determined, we'd finally have the home of our dreams. As I walked in, I prayed that I had done all that I could do and now it was all in God's hands. The only thing I remember is that when I walked in, Salami was sitting with the banker and he smiled, letting me know that I had made it in time and the house now belonged to us.

Only God could have known every need we had and foresaw the plans he had for us. Every day I am thankful for this journey I walked with my Fatty. The memories made in our home with our children, grandchildren, family, and friends are my constant reminder that I'm exactly where I'm supposed to be.

Linda Espinoza lives in Firebaugh, California. She is the mother of three, grandmother of four. Believer and follower of Jesus Christ. Linda is working on her first book, Tell Your Heart to Beat Again; Allow Your Brokenness to Become Your Breakthrough. If you want to contact Linda, you can reach her at lindaespn@yahoo.com.

Salami and Linda at the auction, September 11, 2013

Angels Among Us

CHAPTER 3
TOUCHED BY AN ANGEL

Tragedy Averted
Craig Amos

This story occurred in the winter of 1987. I was twenty-one years old, a newlywed and an up-and-coming pastor who was serving in youth ministry and working full-time for a medical oxygen company as an o2 technician. My life was busy and fast paced due to various commitments, so I was always on the go.

As I was driving in my work truck along Taft Highway outside of Bakersfield, California, on a cold and foggy morning, I had what I consider to be divine intervention.

I accidentally fell asleep for perhaps five to seven seconds while driving approximately fifty-five to sixty miles per hour with an oxygen tank bolted to the back of my truck bed. I was jolted out of my sleep because I felt someone tap me on my left shoulder three times. The taps were prominent, forceful, and distinct. I woke up just as I was about to plow into the car right in front of me. I immediately slammed on my brakes and still rear-ended the vehicle in front of me, but I have no doubt that I applied the brakes just in time before the accident could have been much, much worse, even deadly.

Over three decades later, there is still no question in my mind that something, or someone touched me. I know exactly what I felt.

Thankfully no one was severely hurt in the accident in either vehicle. I got out of the car without a scratch and even though my truck was smashed all the way to the steering wheel, I believe tragedy was averted. I believe that it was an angel of the Lord that woke me up just in time. It was not my time to go. Scripture says in Psalm 91:11, "For He shall give His angels charge over you, to keep you in all your ways."

Rev. Craig Amos serves as Lead Pastor of CityView Church (A Canyon Hills Campus) in Bakersfield, California at 3535 Union Avenue. He has been ordained Assemblies of God minister for over thirty years and has pastored several churches in California and the Midwest. Craig has also served as a hospice chaplain for the last sixteen years. He and his wife, Angie, have been married for over thirty-five years and they have two grown children and two beautiful grandchildren. He was saved at nineteen years of age after witnessing the tragic drunk driving death of his young neighbor who was just twenty-four years old. Craig holds both a bachelor's degree in theology and master's degree in pastoral counseling. For inquiries about his ministry, email craig@canyonhills.com

A Helping Hand
John Warner

When I was growing up, scouting was a big part of my life. I was a member of Troop 80 of the First Methodist Church in Pampa, Texas. I became an Eagle Scout.

My Scoutmaster was Flaudie Gallman. He worked at the Cargray Gasoline Plant about fifteen miles west of Pampa. We would often camp out over a weekend at Cargray. That way Mr. Gallman could oversee us during his lunch hour and after work. When he was at work, we were without adult supervision.

One time when Mr. Gallman was working, the other scouts and I decided to cut steps from the top of a cliff down to a dry river bottom. It was a foolish and foolhardy thing to attempt, but we did not think the project through.

We soon learned that the cliff was too steep for steps. We then decided to cut steps from one part of the cliff to the other. I don't remember if I volunteered or was chosen to test our steps.

I started down the side of the cliff. It went almost straight down. I slipped and began to fall. As I fell, the thought, "God will save me," flashed through my mind.

It was almost as if a hand lifted me back up on that ledge. My right foot caught on a crumbly edge of the cliff. I regained my balance and was able to scramble to safety.

The next time we were there, the crumbly edge of the cliff which I had stepped on had fallen down into the dry river bottom below.

To this day I do not see any way that crumbly edge held my weight and allowed me to regain my balance. I believe that God directly intervened in my life that day and saved me.

John Warner is a bestselling author of the popular small group study guides: Bible Study Lessons: Weekly Plans for Church Leaders - Volumes one through four. He is also an attorney for over sixty years. He has also taught Sunday School and coached little league baseball for over fifty years. He is dedicated to his wife, family and community. For more info, email: jww_pampa@yahoo.com.

Jesus, Take the Wheel
Denise Hoole

Several years ago, my son, Tyler, was killed in a car accident that was a result of distracted driving. He was less than a mile from home. Since then, I have always been a little worried when I have to drive a long distance as there are so many cars on the road. There are so many people on their phones or not paying attention to the road!

I live in California, which is notorious for traffic. I was driving on the I-5 from Fresno to San Diego (which is about a seven-hour drive) and taking the same route I always do.

I was at the end of a long drive, almost into downtown San Diego when suddenly - my car was struck by a SUV out of nowhere. The car automatically pushed me into the fast lane and I hit the SUV that was coming from that lane on my driver's side.

All I could see was that the car that originally hit me, spun from hitting me. I didn't have any mirrors left on my car, so I could not see any of the other cars or where to pull over. All of sudden, a sense of calm came over me. I felt this incredible peace and it felt like someone else took the steering wheel and was driving my car.

I called out Tyler's name, saying "Tyler" over and over again. I was able to get off the highway to a safe spot. I don't really know how I avoided getting hit by oncoming cars and traffic without any mirrors. I should have been more injured and should not have been able to get off the highway in one piece. It was literally as if my car had wings and smoothly and calmly was able to exit the danger.

Tyler was with me, gently guiding me to safety, even when I could not see other cars around me.

Once I was safe, I started screaming and crying - realizing how close I came to certain injury or death. I wondered if Tyler felt the same comfort or fear when he had his accident? I was shaking so hard as I realized that he had saved me from a similar fate.

I called my boyfriend and my kids and was so grateful to hear their voices. Thank you, Tyler, for keeping me safe. I always ask Tyler, my parents, God & Jesus to watch over me when I am driving a long distance. I definitely had some special angels watching over me that day.

Denise Hoole lives in the San Diego area with her kids. She is also an advocate against distracted driving and donor awareness. To book Denise as a speaker, she can be reached via email: hooledenise1973@gmail.com

CHAPTER 4
CHILDREN AND ANGELS

Through the Eyes of a Child
Lo Anne Mayer

As a military child in 1946 we lived on an army base in Texas. After having been diagnosed with asthma, I had several bouts with pneumonia and was finally hospitalized in an army hospital that had no pediatric ward. I was placed in a ward near a nurses' station where I was one of the first to receive a new medicine called penicillin. At the time penicillin only came in the form of a shot. I was scared to death! When my mother was told I had to stay overnight, I was even more terrified because she could not stay. The nurse assured us that she would be "right next door" and would come at a moment's notice if I needed anything.

Because my father was commandant of the base and was very much a rule follower, he convinced my mother that everything would be alright as he took her home. After pushing the button for a nurse on several occasions and receiving no response, I started to cry. I cried myself to sleep after the nurse that came told me to go to sleep in her most authoritarian voice. After that I cried more softly but the tears kept coming. I remembered a prayer that my mother taught me, and I said that prayer over and over. "Angel of God, my guardian dear, to whom God's love commits me here. Ever this night be at my side to light, to guard, to rule and guide. Amen." Eventually, I drifted off to a fitful sleep.

Sometime in the night I woke up to see some friends in the crib-type bed that I had been placed in. My "friends" were lit up like Christmas lights and brought games to play. I don't know how long we played games, but I felt happy and safe with them. When I felt sleepy, my friends said that they would wait as I fell asleep. I remember one of them covered me with a blanket and kissed me goodnight.

The next morning, I woke up feeling much better when my mother came into the hospital room. I tried to tell her about my friends, but the doctor was talking to her, so no one really paid attention to my rambling. Looking back, I know now that angels came to visit me in the form of children. They were lit up like Christmas lights for me because they knew Christmas was coming and I was excited about going to my grandmother's for the holidays. They created a safe and comfortable environment for me to sleep. I didn't call them angels. I called them friends, which was exactly what they were!

Fast forward to 2006. Our daughter, Cyndi, died tragically the year before. My eight-year-old grandson recovered from cancer thanks to good medicine and lots of prayer. We were so happy that he was past all the surgery and chemo and was now living a normal life.

One day our daughter, Karen, called me to say that I needed to speak to Graham because he had a question that she couldn't answer. She put him on the phone, and this was his question: "What is the difference between angels and ghosts?" Before I answered, I asked him why he wanted to know. I thought he had watched a scary movie and I wanted to answer him appropriately. His response completely floored me. "Well Cyndi hangs out in my sister's room all the time and I don't know whether she is a ghost or an angel." Over the years I had done lots of research on angels. I even taught a class, Ask Your Angels, for seven years, so I felt qualified to answer the question.

I told Graham that angels had been created by God in order to help humans remember that God loves them and wanted them to have a companion to help them live their lives and to bring them back home to Him when they die. Angels never lived in a human body but could be seen by humans, especially children, on occasion and are here to serve God and man. Ghosts on the other hand previously lived as humans and sometimes appear to people because the ghost needs help or it has a message for the human being. All Graham said was "Ok, I get it." He was about to hang up when I asked Graham, "Have you ever seen an angel?" He reacted immediately with a firm "Yes."

44

"Really?" I responded. Graham and I had spent many hours together while he was going through his cancer treatment. He never mentioned angels to me during all that time.

"When did you see angels?"

"When I had my surgeries. I saw lots of them."

"How come you never mentioned that to me?" I responded.

"You never asked me," he said and quickly added that he had to go.

My phone was still in my hand as I thought back to all the months we had been together during his illness. He was right. I never mentioned angels. I never asked if he saw them. I missed an important conversation. Don't you miss the chance to discuss angels with the little ones. They can teach you so much.

Lo Anne is the author of Celestial Conversations: Healing Relationships After Death. She is in the process of writing her second book, The Treasures in Grief: Discover 7 Spiritual Gifts Hidden in Your Pain. Her website is www.CelestialConversations.com and you can reach her at lamayer@msn.com.

A Gentle Kiss and the Celebration of Angels
Greg Sanders

Becky had to leave soon. She was also upset.

Darren, her ten-year-old nephew and our oldest son, was sleeping or unresponsive and had not talked or made eye contact the whole day. Because he had a fatal illness in the final stages, she knew that after she left for Michigan, she would never see him again. She had just wanted to say good-bye. She wondered, "How can I let him know how much I love him? How much I will miss him?"

Becky moved her face closer to Darren's to study the face of this darling boy for the last time. His eyes were still closed. That's when the miracle occurred.

The kiss. She didn't ask for it. She didn't initiate it. Darren did, or God did. That part is unclear to her. She only knows that with that gentle, honest kiss, a miracle happened, and heaven and the world of angels appeared to her sight.

Before I describe Becky's vision, let me introduce you to Darren, a brave boy with an aggressive form of acute lymphocytic leukemia illness who possessed a fierce love for God and all people, and an extraordinary faith. I will also tell you about how he opened up the world of God and unconditional love to many other people.

Darren Cristofer Sanders was a precocious child, reading letters off car license plates at age eighteen months, knowing all of his colors, shapes, and letters about the same time, and reading The Hobbit and other advanced books at the age of five. This is the same age that most kids are nailing down the alphabet and colors. Darren especially loved the color purple.

He also loved all people of all ages. His mother Karen and I were amazed at his maturity in relating to people, and his empathy. He seemed to sense the emotional states of others.

When Darren was eighteen months old, Grandma Jane was riding in the back seat with Darren on a long road trip. Her back was sore. Darren seemed to sense his grandma's discomfort and let her know that he was concerned for her. She clearly remembers his uncanny empathy. What child cares about the comfort of adults before the age of two and has the ability to express that concern?

Darren was also a kind older brother to his siblings, David, Melody, Tiffany and Dwight. When Darren was five years old and holding newborn Tiffany he said profoundly, "Babies sure fill your heart up with love." He saw the wondrous nature of the spark of life in all of us.

Darren contracted leukemia just as he turned five, lost his curly golden hair, and started a different life than most kids. He studied in "home school," wore a little gray cap to cover his bald head when he left the house, went to special support cancer camps for kids, and adapted to being a "leukemia kid." He not only adapted to limitations, he seemed to thrive. He even wrote a little booklet about leukemia to explain it to others, with drawings.

His normal life may have been filled with hospitals and needles, but in his mental life, he thrived. After I created one kid-simplified booklet of The Lion, The Witch and The Wardrobe, Darren started creating his own books and stories. He helped me create several board games - The Black Cauldron, Treasure Chest (a Bible game), The Hobbit (of course), and he helped with the artwork and creating hand-drawn, decorative pieces. He also created a life-like image of Smaug the Dragon with colored glass in plaster, along with many other pieces of art.

Darren was in and out of hospitals from age five to eight, but finally the cancer seemed to disappear. Not a trace of "blasts" anywhere in his blood. We were all excitely hopeful. He started living a normal life apart from being a "leukemia kid" and had a bright future. Then at age nine, after seventeen months of remission, Darren suffered a full relapse. The leukemia returned, and odds of survival dropped from fifty percent to ten percent. We were all disappointed, but we redoubled our prayers. Many people started praying for Darren's complete recovery.

Grandma Lorraine recalls a night spent with Darren in the hospital in Lansing, Michigan. "Grandma," said Darren, "we need to pray." You would think he might pray for himself, for his own recovery. Nope. Darren felt the urgency of praying for others. Darren prayed for the doctors and nurses, and others. He suddenly stopped praying, and Grandma looked up at him and saw a glow in the room and felt a strong sense of God's presence. After a few moments, Darren opened his eyes and simply said, "Good night, grandma." And that was that.

The nurses often told us how they loved having Darren as a patient, how polite and kind he was, how cooperative he was for pokes and procedures, how they loved talking to him, almost friend to friend. Nurses said that they "had a better day" when they could visit with him,

47

or even walk by his room and peek through the glass. Sometimes they would place their hands on the glass for a few moments, as if to impart or receive a blessing. Everyone agreed there was just something special about Darren.

Despite the relapse, we still "knew" that God would heal him, even if it took miracles. The first "miracle" happened when a new bone marrow transplant unit opened in St. Louis Children's Hospital, just as we were moving to the area. Then came the second miracle. The transplant unit would only take patients with a sibling matched bone marrow donor. Tiffany, age four, the little sister who "fills your heart with love," turned out to be a perfect match. We were convinced this was God's answer for healing. Appropriately, Tiffany's middle name is Hope.

We had unshakeable faith in God to heal Darren. Darren also had faith, but he also knew the seriousness of his illness. At one point he (age eight or nine) and David (next in line, age seven) were talking. "David," said Darren. "You know the story of how Elijah gave his mantle (cloak) to Elisha?" "Yeah," said David, "What about it?" Darren replied, "Well, if I die and go to heaven, I'm going to give you my mantle so that you'll be in charge." The implication was that David could be the leader of the other kids and watch out for them. "No thanks," said David, "You can keep it."

Darren had determined to read the whole Bible from cover to cover. He had finished the Old Testament, the four gospels and Acts, and was reading the book of Romans, a book full of deep theology. My neighbor Brian tells of when he was leaving church one Sunday. People were streaming out of the building, parting like the Red Sea around a small ten-year-old boy sitting on the steps, reading his Bible. Darren was oblivious to the swarm of humanity passing him by. When the crowd thinned, Brian walked down the steps and sat down by Darren.

"What are you reading?" he asked, expecting a young boy's answer, "I'm reading the Bible," or maybe, "I'm reading the New Testament." Instead he got an answer that let him know that he was sitting by a pure soul who clearly understood the deep reality of God's love. Darren looked up, "I'm reading the place in Romans where God justified Abraham by faith." His golden hair was gone and a hat covered his bald head, but his face was glowing. Brian said he felt like he was in the presence of a spiritual giant, far advanced beyond his age.

One of the things that I miss most about Darren was his beautiful, angelic voice. Darren could sing! I still remember his boy soprano voice soaring over the congregational singing. He often sang solos in church, including "I Love You, Lord," a song that combined a pure, sweet voice with a heartfelt passion for Jesus. At the age of nine, he was asked to narrate the biblical Christmas story for the whole church play. He willingly agreed. He had no fear of large crowds whether he was speaking or singing.

In October of 1991, his best friend Kyle, from Kalamazoo, Michigan, came for a visit. Kyle asked, "Darren, what is it like to know that you might die?" Darren said, "Well, Kyle, I would just go to heaven and help prepare a place for you." Darren converted his friend's worry and concern for himself into faith and hope.

The bone marrow transplant was technically a success, but the chemo was overwhelming his liver. His belly became bloated and uncomfortable. He could hardly turn over, and he had to sleep on his side. The weeks dragged on, and things were getting worse. We eagerly clung to hope, but the doctors could give us none. We all wanted Darren to get better, and he himself was eager to be home for Thanksgiving, a few short weeks away. We didn't know it at the time, but Darren did not have long to live.

Let's return to Becky's story as she was trying to say good-bye to her unresponsive nephew. As a medically trained PT, she clearly could see that Darren was dying and these were her last moments with him on this earth. She was out of time, and out of options.

She felt she couldn't leave without a meaningful connection. She prayed silently but said nothing. Darren must have sensed her emotional confusion even as he lay there quietly. As she put her head close to his, Darren's hand reached out and pulled her closer into a gentle kiss with his swollen, cracked lips on hers. She was surprised but grateful that she didn't have to leave without saying good-bye.

When their lips met, Becky said she instantly saw a vision. She sensed it was the same vision that Darren was also seeing, of a group of angels rejoicing. They were celebrating his coming arrival to heaven. No words were spoken, but Becky could tell that Darren wanted to go with them, but the angels told him it was not yet time. "Soon," they said. What Becky noticed most was that the angels were so animated, joyful, and so very happy. The word "excited" doesn't begin to describe their joy. No words could express how happy the angels were that they would soon be the escorts for this young man of faith to his heavenly home. She also knew that Darren was happy, peaceful, and had no fear of dying. He was ready to go. When Darren ended the kiss, her vision immediately ended.

It was just a kiss, only a kiss. Yet it opened up the world of heaven to her inner sight. It was only a few moments, yet it was powerful and gave her a deep peace that had previously eluded her. For a long time she was not able to talk about the experience.

The next day, on the Wednesday evening before God took him home, Darren was restless in his bed. His belly was greatly swollen beyond its normal size, and he could only sleep on his side so he wouldn't suffocate. His nurse Linea asked, "Darren, when you are lying there with your eyes closed, do you ever see anything?"

He said quietly, "Yes. I see Jesus in the light. And He told me I will be well."

That was November 20, 1991, a few days before Thanksgiving. Darren really, really wanted to go home before Thanksgiving. He had it marked on his calendar, circled in red.

Up until the day before he died, I still held out hope that God would heal Darren completely. I could see no reason why God would create such a miraculous child, give him a coveted place in a new bone marrow ward for kids, and give him a sister as a perfect donor match, only to take his life. What a waste, I thought. Why would God allow that? But the doctors told us on Thursday that Darren had no chance of making it.

On that Friday morning, I was by Darren's side, helplessly watching his fight for life. Karen was there also, as were some nurses. We all felt helpless. I would have traded the world for this valiant young boy to live. He was a spiritual giant in my eyes even though he was a child.

As he swung his arms, fighting for breath, I felt a spiritual presence in the room, powerful yet peaceful. The thought and impression came to me strongly, "Release him. Tell him that I'm waiting," the thoughts came to me unbidden.

It was the hardest thing that I had yet done in my life. With tears in my eyes I said, "Darren, it's okay. You can go to Jesus now. He's waiting." Within moments, my son, my first-born, my angel on earth, relaxed and became peaceful and still. He had gone to be with his Lord. His fight, his journey, his ten bright years on earth, were over. Darren, like Abraham, had been "justified by faith," and the best chapters of his life were just beginning. The thought came to me. It's not how long we live that matters; it's how brightly we shine.

We were grieving and felt acute loss, yet Darren's confidence and faith still comforted us.

The funeral in Greenville was attended by hundreds. People expected a child's funeral to be a sad event, even tragic. As they supported us in our grief, they found a joyful celebration of life for a remarkable child of God. There was joyous, faith-filled music and powerful tributes by family members and even some of his nurses. His own recorded voice sang, "I Love You, Lord." It was a powerful moment. Many commented later on how moved they were, even those who had never met Darren.

After the service, his aunt Becky and grandma Lorraine walked out and saw a solitary balloon above the church, rising upward, higher and higher. "Where did that balloon come from?" they wondered. No one knew. The balloon was purple, Darren's favorite color, the color of royalty, the color of the King of Kings.

The church in Williamston, Michigan, also had a memorial tribute for Darren. This church was led by Darren's grandfather, Dwight Knasel, and had been praying for many months. A colorful balloon bouquet had been placed in his honor at the front of the church. During the final hymn, one solitary balloon broke free from the others and floated up to the peak of the ceiling.

Grandma Lorraine later brought the deflated balloon to us. The balloon was purple.

There is a tapestry to God's work, a pattern that none of us could have created alone. Each person had one or two pieces of the puzzle. None of us saw the whole picture until we started sharing stories. God revealed himself through Darren to each of us in a different way. Angels brought a beautiful soul to earth, and in God's timing, angels took him home to heaven, celebrating all the way.

Darren himself was like an "angel among us." He loved God, served others, and showed us a pure picture of God's nature. He showed us what true faith is like as we face death.

I imagine that when we get to heaven, Darren will take us to see the mansion he helped make for Kyle. He may even have one for us! We look forward to that day. I wouldn't be surprised if the front door isn't decorated with a purple balloon!

Dr. Greg Sanders and his wife Karen have lost three children to leukemia, heart disease, and mental illness. Darren was the first. They have four surviving children and a great faith in God. Greg was a university professor for thirty years, has a PhD in sociology, and is the founder of The Max Community, an online business network. https://TheMaxCommunity.com

Darren (8), Melody (6), Tiffany (4), Grandpa Elliot and David (7)

Darren (age 4) and Becky

Brotherly Love
Melanie Warner

I was pregnant with my third child, Carson, and remember how I felt when I walked into my dream home for the first time. I had a strong vision of three kids playing in the backyard, presumably Carson and his older sister and brother.

As I was touring the house, one of the rooms had a mural of angels on it. They had been painted by a local artist and her son. He was well-known as a young artist in our hometown and had sold paintings to pay for his expensive medical treatments as he battled leukemia. I knew, instantly, that would be Carson's room.

We closed escrow on the house just before I went into the hospital to give birth to Carson.

During delivery, the hospital made some critical errors that compromised Carson's life and almost cost me my life. My uterus ruptured as well as four major arteries that led to it. I was in danger of bleeding out, but Carson's position in my body actually saved my life. As a result, he had been without oxygen for almost thirty minutes. He was born with a brain injury and went into a coma. I was inconsolable when we had to make the horrific decision to take him off of life support and he passed away.

For years, I felt like someone was always missing in our family. How could that vision be so strong in our home to include three kids if Carson didn't ever get to come home from the hospital or be in his room?

We wanted another child and looked into adoption and even contemplated surrogacy. Nothing was working out for us, so I surrendered to the fact that I would probably not have another child. I was grateful for the two that I had - and that they were healthy. I donated all of my maternity clothes and Carson's baby items. It was time to let go.

Then, a week later - I found out I was pregnant! I was overjoyed at this miracle of life that I didn't think was possible.

Almost three years to the day, my little miracle boy, Hudson Carson Kennedy, came into this world. When we brought him home from the hospital, his room became the room that had originally been Carson's. It brought me so much peace to be in that room and gently rock him to sleep as I sat under the murals of angels and hope.

One day, when Hudson was about a year old, I walked by his room and heard him babbling in his little baby voice. He was just talking in gibberish like babies do. He was in his crib, looking up and just talking away to someone.

"Who are you talking to? I asked him, without expecting an answer.

He looked right at me in his little baby voice and said, "Carson."

My eyes flooded with tears as my heart warmed at the thought of the two of them chatting away in Carson's room. I had never discussed his brother with him. He was, after all, a baby and barely able to talk or put words together. I didn't feel the need to tell him about his brother until he was older.

But my spirit was lifted knowing that they had already met and bonded in this special way that only children can appreciate and not fear.

Melanie Warner is the founder and publisher of the Defining Moments book series. She loves having a platform to help people share inspiring and uplifting stories. She also helps people write, publish and launch a book. She can be reached at:
melanie@mydefiningmoments.com For more info on sharing your story, or writing your own book, visit: www.MyDefiningMoments.com

Angels Among Us

CHAPTER 5

VISIONS AND LIGHT

Protection
Jackie Leach

I worked with a woman in Houston, Texas who shared her remarkable story with me. She was on a plane and had experienced extreme turbulence, so she began to pray. When the storm ended, there was a beautiful rainbow in the sky above the clouds. She quickly pulled out her camera and took a photo of the rainbow from her seat on the plane.

This was many years back before digital cameras where you can see the photo instantly. She took her film to be developed, and when she received her photos back - she was shocked at what she saw.

Instead of the rainbow, there was a white outline of Jesus Christ in the photo. She could even see the holes in his hands and his feet where he had been nailed to the cross, with light shining through from the clouds behind Him. He had his hands out as if to say, "I'm here with you."

She brought the photo to work and shared it with all of us. She gave me an extra copy to keep. It had a profound effect on my faith as a young Mom. Shortly after, she moved away and we lost touch.

I decided to make copies of the photo she gave me. When I went back to pick them up, the man who worked there said the photo disappeared and they could not find it anywhere. They had lost it!

I was disappointed that they lost my photo, but I think about it often. Any time I have fear, I always know the true power of who is walking next to me. It strengthened my faith and validated for me that God is always with us - no matter what.

Jackie Leach is a retired mother and grandmother who lives in Katy, Texas. She has a personal relationship with her Lord Jesus Christ and attends church regularly.

Don't Just See It, Feel It
Keri Faith Knudtson

"Don't just see it, feel it."

This was the guidance and advice received from family and friends who had previously visited the holy land in Israel.

Prior to traveling in July 2022, I knew that I would be 'cracked open' during this adventure but I didn't quite know how.

My friends reminded me to not just see the sights of Israel but to also feel them.

It was like any other day up until this point in Israel; I was experiencing jet lag with an on-the-go itinerary and little time to rest. I just wanted to take in as many sights as possible.

Just a few days prior, I had left written prayers in the cracks of the Western Wall, a common custom in the holy land. In these prayers I specifically asked God to guide me, to allow me to feel abundant, and create abundance, prosperity, and expansion around me.

The hot early morning sun (which was rising in the far East while approaching the Western Bank) ushered in the abundance I was seeking. Sounds of celebration in the streets from horns to fireworks, to ringing bells filled the air. Once a year, high school students receive their scores for college entrance exams and celebrate their passing to arrive upon the next step of their life's journey. And this was the day.

Some of the most profound pops of fireworks frightened my soul as the noise echoed like gunshots across the valley of the West Bank.

Visiting Bethlehem, Israel with my husband, son, daughter, parents, sister, brother-in-law, and nephews for the first time with sounds of explosions and blasts distilled a type of fear that I hadn't experienced up until now in the holy land.

Quite honestly, the fear was unsettling. Our paid local Palestinian guide assured us that the frightening pops were fireworks but how was I to know? Most people's fear and rightful concern mixed with ignorance of traveling in the Middle East were projected upon me and rising to the surface of my gut and chest.

Over the past week in Israel, we saw fights, protestors, and the contrast of living conditions from the bustling nightlife in Tel Aviv to the majestic ruins in Masada, and the evaporating, sizzling hot Dead Sea in July.

It was Shabbat, and our family was rapidly approaching the Holy Trinity Church of Nativity as our guide was quickly rushing us through the streets of Bethlehem. The sun glaring behind the Holy Trinity sculpture was the perfect primer and representation of what was to come.

I was protected here by shade and something much larger than life. Much bigger than you or I.

I wasn't sure what to expect at the birthplace of Jesus. I previously had not studied the bible by any means as I was raised in a Reformed Jewish family without a religious foundation besides the traditions of Judaism that generations and generations had previously practiced.

The first of three secular churches inside the Holy Trinity Church of Nativity, I cleansed with Holy Water and shared my prayers. My husband and I were the only ones that took that moment to cleanse and pray, opening ourselves up to something beyond what we envisioned was possible by honoring God in His holy place.

Next it was the elaborate and decorated Islamic Armenian Church. We were shuffled to the waiting quarter to visit the historical marker of Jesus' birth. It was small, dark, and cool on this heated summer day. Quite the contrast from what most people imagine after reading the Bible and routinely seeing replicas of the manger inspired by historical text. The stairway to the cave is narrow, cobblestone, and people squished together to observe one of the holiest places on earth, the very place that His life began. Walking down the narrow stairway into the cave there were probably fifty people being rushed to take a quick snapshot and be pushed out. But for me, I knew there was something more than just a photograph of the star.

So, I walked to the very far corner of the cave, to the darkest and quietest corner in the bustling excitement that some people wait their entire lives to witness.

I paused.

I remembered the words, "Don't just see it, feel it."

I placed one knee on the ground, like I was proposing to a new marriage without a ring but with the loyalty that I would be bound for life, and put both hands on the cool cobblestone floor, proceeded to close both eyes.

Within a millisecond of closing my eyes the brightest white light engulfed my very being and essence. It was the purest and whitest light that I have ever seen. This white light rushed throughout my entire body, engulfing my heart, and circled me above, below, and all around. It was angelic! Tears started rushing down my face. I wasn't expecting to feel this way. I had no idea that this type of light existed at all let alone in darkness with my eyes shut.

The very same bright white light that I experienced is depicted in the Manger's Scene.

I had no idea until I looked back, that it was the same northern light showing over Jesus at birth.

I believe that the northern light exists within you. In the same way that the northern star guided the wise men to Jesus, there is a light inside of all of us that recognizes and guides us to God, if we are open.

I met the son of God that day. Me, a Jew, born in La Jolla, California met Jesus Christ and discovered He was more than a man. He's the son of God.

I didn't see Him, but I felt Him. And every day since I have felt the love He has for me, and the love I now hold for Him. That day was the start of the most transformative spiritual journey of my life.

I no longer just have a job or career; I have the mission to share that light. That light is the powerful love of the God that you can access from the moment you wake until the moment you sleep.

I also have the understanding that when I feel anxious, worried, lonely, or confused, unseen or unheard, or like I lack something (scarcity), God is there for me. He hears me and He guides me in many different ways. Because I am His child.

I am acutely aware of the many angels and directional signs that it took to be here. Every single person that played a role in getting me to that place at that exact moment, to experience the most powerful encounter of my life was an angel. Never underestimate your ability to impact the life of another and share God's light when you are open to receiving it. We can all be an angel in the life of someone else when you are led by feeling and experiencing the light from within.

Keri Faith Knudtson is an Author, Speaker, and Transformational Leadership Coach. She empowers women to BE the Leader they were born to BE so they can confidently earn more money doing what they love. She helps her clients build strategic brand identity, culture, and leadership through entrepreneurship endeavors.

Additional Links:
Instagram: www.instagram.com/kerifaithonpurpose/
Podcast: Keri Faith on Purpose on Apple Podcasts

The Holy Spirit Trinity Church

An Angel Beside Me
Rita Gladding

The loss of a child, while unbelievable, swiftly becomes undeniable. The connection between mothers that have lost a child has strong ties. We become infected with it like a disease. Mothers "get" each other. We support one another while silently, fervently praying for the return of our child. Always knowing that will never transpire. Not in a human state, nevertheless. The members of this group look for signs from God that the child we believe is lost is not lost at all. They are gone from this planet but exist on another plane. They are angels among us.

My book, *Gavin...Gone, Turning Pain into Purpose to Create a Legacy* is the story of the tragic loss of my son. As a mother I was always terrified of being the recipient of the ominous phone call that my husband and I received via car phone on a beautiful Sunday morning. The call no parent ever wants to take. It was our daughter, Gabrielle. As she began to speak, I could hear background noises from the road. She was traveling somewhere. Innocently, I answer my cell phone. "Hi. What's happening?" She immediately cuts me off. She is talking fast. "Mom, there's been an accident. It's Gavin." I could hear panic in her voice. "Come directly to the emergency room at Community Regional Medical Center downtown.

Do not go home." Those few, uncomplicated words twisted my life in the direction of a path I never anticipated to travel down.

Gavin had been the victim of a hit-and-run accident while training for his third marathon. Hit from behind, others training for the event became eyewitnesses. They watched his body fly through the air (Gavin was six feet tall). Even today, I find it difficult to label his death an accident. The driver of the truck along with his passenger consciously made a dreadful decision to leave the human being they had struck by the side of the road. As the truck sped away, the closest runner reached Gavin. He was still breathing. When we reached the Emergency Room, we were told that in the few moments it had taken an ambulance to reach the scene, Gavin had died. My strong faith convinces me that God wanted him. Needed him to be beside him above. The three runners twenty feet behind Gavin were spared. He was the chosen one. An angel among us forever more.

Immediate unimaginable raw grief launches the nightmare we have lived for the past four years. There are people who walk this earth capable of heinous acts. They are without consciences or souls. The killers hid out for five days. The Fresno County Highway patrol launched their largest investigation for Gavin's killers in the last ten years. We took deep breaths in and out and prayed they would be successful. In the long run the three involved in Gavin's death were apprehended. Bringing them to justice became another story.

This was the time that Gavin's spirit began to reach our entire valley. News of his death spread like a wildfire. Front page news. Our local newspaper, The Fresno Bee, headlines read, "Clovis educator killed while jogging in hit-and-run crash." For the next nine months more headlines continued regularly. "Family pleads for hit-and-run driver who killer educator to turn self in"; "Driver who killed Clovis school official pleads no contest – had no driver's license -remains free on bail; and the most devastating headline: "Clovis school official was still alive after being struck by driver." This was also the moment when a mother of a past student of his while he taught Advanced Placement Environmental Science to high schoolers, took a bold step forward. Prompted by her son, she requested, then collected over ninety-seven letters written by students when they learned of Gavin's senseless death. The book, He Loved Us –

Stories of Mr. Gladding from the Students Who Loved Him, is an overwhelming account of the priceless thoughts and opinions of children he educated. Heart wrenching letters filled with praise for a young teacher who had been taken from this Earth entirely too soon. Described as kind, supportive, caring, devoted, having a positive impact on students, an amazing human being – Gavin was a perfect candidate to become an angel. He was called Adboulraxman, meaning 'The Messenger from God,' by the villagers in Africa when he arrived as a Peace Corps volunteer. The significance was clear - he was to become a messenger from God. An angel among us.

Gavin was a pure soul. Announcing in the seventh grade that he intended to attend the University of California Santa Barbara before living on the land, he kept both promises. Earning a degree in Environmental Science from UCSB he immediately joined the Peace Corps to spend two years as a volunteer in the West African country of The Gambia. This, the third poorest country on the African continent, is where his life as an educator began. In a mud hut with nothing but a dirt floor, working with children who had limited grasp of the English language. He was completely at ease teaching the children in his village of Charmen. Returning to the United States Gavin knew how he wanted to spend his life – as an instructor, engaging young minds to use their brains, enlarge their frame of references, to think.

Our family spent eight months in and out of the Fresno County Courthouse as the three killers managed to stay free on bail to wait for their day in court. For us, it wasn't pretty. As the murderers were given lenient sentences, little to no jail time, it was evident the criminal justice system clearly failed us in our hometown. We began to think outside the box for a way to be certain Gavin's legacy would live on. Setting two goals we established a non-profit foundation in Gavin's name to grant college scholarships to graduating high school seniors. To achieve this goal, we committed to honor him yearly with a fundraising golf tournament. Our triumphant success in this task has allowed us to fund college scholarships; plus provide major support for the River Parkway Trust and Conservatory's River Camp program (Gavin worked with them intermittently for fifteen years – five of which were spent as head of the camp) and join forces with another non-profit, GambiaRising which provides funding and food for mostly high school girls in The Gambia. His legacy will continue to thrive.

Then the final goal. We pursued a statewide effort to change the law regarding terms of imprisonment for hit-and-run drivers. AB 582 Gavin's Law. From March 2019 (six months after he was killed) through November 2022, we have made numerous trips led by our local Assemblyman to Sacramento to achieve this second goal. We are due to return in the spring of 2023 to continue the pursuit still seeking justice for Gavin. I feel he is beside us in the cold courtrooms of the state capitol building. We will take him with us on every appearance we make. Gavin was about fairness and justice. This is what his human persona was. Now I sense it descending from above.

I recognize 'sensing' his presence isn't enough. As a Catholic, I don't have blind faith. I believe in the teachings of the Bible and in Jesus Christ. My beliefs are real. I know Gavin will not physically return. However, I still want proof with all my heart that he does return as an angel during settings that he should have been a part of. Courtrooms where we have fought for justice for him. Events that we founded for him. Always conscious he is with us on all holidays as an angel – as the messenger from God. In spirit, not in body.

Our family had experienced other hiccups along our journey through life. After not being able to conceive a second child, the hand of God reached down to deliver to us a perfect baby girl to adopt. I believe it was that same hand of God that reached down to pick Gavin up off the side of the road, covered with his own blood, and take him to Heaven.

The first accounting of Gavin returning as an angel was four days after his death on Sunday, September 16, 2018. Gary had been inconsolable for these four days. On Thursday morning September 20th, I reached the kitchen to see him smiling at me. I wasn't sure what to expect. Exposing his clean soul he said to me, "I'm fine. I had an epiphany in the middle of the night. I woke up, sat up and Gavin was sitting right next to me. He told me everything would be ok."

As Fort Washington Elementary School dedicated their 2018 - 2019 yearbook to Gavin they had put together a compilation of pictures of him over his two years as their Vice-Principal. As the entire student body sat on the floor to look at the slide show, the only sounds in the room to be heard were the soft sobs coming from these students that loved him. The last picture was accompanied by Israel Kamakawiwo'ole's Hawaiian version of the song Over the Rainbow. The staff at Fort Washington knew where he was. It was the most beautiful send off. He was indeed, and forever, over the rainbow.

The accompanying photograph was taken the morning of our first Gavin Gladding Foundation Golf Tournament held to raise the funds to continue to sustain his legacy. A sold-out event with 144 golfers in memory and support of Gavin. There was an electric bristle in the air. Energy. His friends from high school, college and fellow teachers turned out to honor him. After a touching speech given by his widow Susan, the immediate Gladding family present gathered together for a group picture. My dear friend Catherine was the standby photographer. The official photographer for the day took the first shot. She says, "Okay - looks good." Then we stayed in place as Catherine asked to take a second picture with her camera. As soon as she looked at her photo she gasped and said, "Rita, you have to see this!" What I looked at was the proof I was seeking to find. A beam of light between my daughter Gabrielle and I shot down from the sky. In the exact place Gavin would be standing if he was still on this Earth. There it was – his appearance as an angel could not be refuted. He is an angel among us.

Two-time breast cancer survivor, Rita lives in Fresno, California with her husband of fifty-one years Gary and remaining child, Gabrielle. She earned a Bachelor of Science degree in Elementary Education at the University of Texas. Her book, Gavin…Gone, Turning Pain into Purpose to Create a Legacy is an Amazon best seller. She can be reached through gavingladdingfoundation.org

Photo taken at Inaugural GGF Golf Tournament, 2019. Note the shaft of light that appears right where Gavin would be standing.

Divine Flight
Oluwatoyin Adeyinka-Emeseh (Pastor Tee)

In December 2020, I had planned to go to Nigeria to see my family after five years of not seeing them, but then Covid hit and many travel restrictions were put in place. One such restriction was that I would have to test negative for Covid a few days prior to my departure. I was excited to see my sister and be with family especially since my mother had passed and been buried in my absence just six months prior. This trip was for me to formally pay my last respects to my mother as the eldest child.

Several days before I was set to fly home, I had the shock of my life: I got Covid and was unable to go! I was completely devastated but still I chose to trust God. Although He does things that we don't understand sometimes, it's okay because He sees the big picture and knows more about any situation that we ever could. In Isaiah chapter 55:8-9, God says "For my thoughts are not your thoughts, neither are your ways my ways, as the heavens are higher than the earth, so are my ways higher than your ways and my thoughts than your thoughts." God knows all things and He is in control of everything. Later He gave me the reasons why He made it to where I couldn't go to Nigeria at this time.

Prayer is a way of life for me so I continued to seek the Lord asking Him when I should plan another trip to Nigeria. In our quiet time together, the Lord would often give me deep revelations on why He was sending me back home, what He had planned.

Fast forward to almost a year after my trip to Nigeria had been canceled, right before my birthday on March 27th, God told me to have a birthday thanksgiving: a celebration of gratitude for my life. I obeyed and it was glorious.

By February of 2022, God had still not released me to go to Nigeria.

I had been praying to God for a year about my trip to Nigeria, whether I should rebook the trip, but he kept saying no. He would give me so many revelations about the work he wanted me to do in Nigeria, but some I could not understand. There were times I would feel frustrated and even angry thinking to myself, "I don't need revelations through dreams about Nigeria, I want to be physically present." I had to remind myself that His ways are not our ways, He knows all things and there is a perfect time for everything.

More than fifteen years ago, God gave me a ministry by the name **Glorious Destinies International Ministry,** a ministry for women and youth. He instructed me that He was sending me to this demographic of people to prepare them in every area as Kingdom soldiers, helping them through His word and revelations to find their purpose.

In February 2022, God spoke to me. He told me that the only way for me to fulfill my purpose is to help others find their purpose, that I had a choice to not listen, but I was reminded of the biblical instruction that we must first choose the kingdom of God and His righteousness and other things will be added to us.

I felt the Lord tell me from that year on that I should have a three-day celebration for the weekend of my March birthday and that I should launch fully into ministry. So, my birthday weekend would be the start of fully launching into ministry. How exciting! He also instructed very loud and clear that on the 27th of March (2022), my birthday, everything that I put on, MUST be white. *"That's an odd request,"* I thought but I chose to trust Him and not lean on my own understanding.

All the while I had been continually praying that God would show me when to bring my ministry work to my home country of Nigeria, but I had not received an answer. From March 2020 to March 2021, it was a clear "no." After March 2021 every time I prayed, I would not receive an answer on whether it was time; it was neither yes nor no.

I kept praying and saying to myself *until He answers me, I am not going* as this has been my policy in trusting God: Trust in the Lord with all your heart, and lean not on your own understanding; In all your ways acknowledge Him, And He shall direct your paths (Proverbs 3:5-6).

On March 27th, 2022, my birthday, I was dressed head to toe in white clothes, my under dresses, dress, hat, and shoes were all white. My birthday fell on a Sunday, so I was at Covenant of Faith Family Church in Fresno California, seated in the back and listening to Pastor Steve Fagbule in an overly exciting and thought-provoking message. Then suddenly the voice of the Holy Spirit told me to take out my phone and take pictures. As a minister who frowns at people using their phones while the message is going, I immediately thought to myself, *"No, that's rude."* But the voice kept coming, so I took out my phone and started to take pictures of the whole church as that is deemed "acceptable" because of social media postings. Then I heard the voice again, *no take pictures of yourself*, so I turned the camera to myself and took selfies. I took pictures of myself from different angles and when I finished, I put the phone away to continue to listen to the message. I didn't touch the phone again during service or at my thanksgiving luncheon.

When I got home later that day, I sat on my bed and took out my phone to look at the different pictures I took. The first picture that came up on my phone was a shock…a mystery. It was a selfie that I had taken that looked strangely distorted. The entire photo was white and there were several images in the photo. One image towards the top of the photo looked like an aircraft. Towards the bottom of the photo there were two squares positioned next to each other. Each square had a black spot inside of it towards the bottom of the square. The two white squares with black at the bottom of them reminded me of a pair of eyes.

"Where is this painting of an aircraft in the church that I have not seen? I didn't take any photos of a plane," I thought to myself.

In a search for answers, I called my pastor and sent him the photo.

"Please I don't understand this picture," I said to him hoping that he could provide some insight or information that I may be overlooking.

All he said was this, "This is a message from God to you."

I told him I knew. That was the only answer to this mystery.

Next, I called my prayer-partner in North Carolina by the name Pastor Rose Afolabi and sent the pictures to her. "My sister, your answers have been given to you, you are free to travel now," she said.

After this call ended, I went into a session of prayers to understand the message God was giving to me from this picture. God who knows all things and answers prayers told me very clearly that this was confirmation of my trip. He said that it was time for me to take the trip and that I would go with His strength and power following me. The time had come for me to go to greater heights, to take flight into higher levels in my ministry. (Literally and figuratively) He said that the plane was taking off that weekend- this made COMPLETE sense because I had officially brought out God's plan for the ministry in a little program that I organized to launch the ministry the day before.

He then showed me that it wasn't an ordinary plane in the image but a "fighter jet." The fighter jet was flying above me with only the pair of "eyes" being visible. God was speaking to me; I felt like He was showing me that all I need is to see Him in everything that I am doing. I knew this was a divine encounter, that He was speaking to me and would continue to speak to me.

The wings were shaped in the way of a fighter jet going with speed for a target. I have a target that God himself has given me, no more crawling or walking, it's time for rapid fight, flight into greater grace and glory with a specific mission in mind.

This encounter was a defining moment in the ministry because it was God confirming that he was taking us to new levels and territory. I was able to experience this connection with God because I was obedient to His instructions even when it didn't make sense. Trusting God is an extremely important part of our walk with Him.

Had I not worn all white and instead wore darker colors like I often do, the photo most certainly would not have come out the way it did. I heeded to the instruction of God and was privileged to have this extraordinary encounter with the King of Kings, the Lord who answers prayers in the way He wants.

In Jeremiah 33:3, we are instructed to pray by asking Him and He will show us great and mighty things. In these great and mighty things are hidden treasures of information and facts which from a natural (not spiritual) point of view may be confusing, even strange. That is why it is so important for us to always ask Him for wisdom and understanding. And always remember that obedience to God brings blessings.

Pastor Oluwatoyin Adeyinka-Emeseh (Pastor Tee) is an ordained servant of the Most High called into the office of prophetic, intercessory and deliverance. She resides in Fresno, California with her husband Henry and two Daughters. Helping youth and women find their identity and purpose through the discovery of God's divine promises is a vision and goal. Pastor Tee's ministry, GLORIOUS DESTINIES INTERNATIONAL MINISTRY, is an international mission to raise end-time soldiers. To contract Pastor Tee email: teegdim@gmail.com

This was one of the selfies that Pastor Tee took at church that day.

This is the distorted selfie and how it turned out. She saw a gold plane in the photo and God shared with her that it was a fighter jet. The "eyes" are at the bottom - as if they were watching the plane.

CHAPTER 6
CLOSE ENCOUNTERS

Grandma Hopper's Butterflies
Curt Ingram

Over the years our family has had an affinity for butterflies, and for good reason. For years we've heard of and personally experienced countless encounters my grandmother, Georgia, had with Monarch Butterflies. Many more than I will mention in this particular story, however, just know that it went well beyond anything we could have ever imagined.

As I turned into Ocean View cemetery with my wife, Donna, and our daughters, Taleah and Taylor, we knew we were running late. I could see the gathering of family and friends across the way, and we were hoping we wouldn't be interrupting the service. This cemetery sits along the Straits of Juan De Fuca and is an absolutely stunning setting. On this particular morning my grandmother, Georgia Spencer, was being laid to rest next to my grandfather, Claude Spencer. As kids, we liked to call him Claude Hopper, so over time he and my grandmother became known as Claude and Georgia Hopper. Yes, they were known as The Hoppers.

I parked the car. As quietly and quickly as we could, we made our way over to the graveside. We were each handed a prayer guide with information about my grandma. It included a beautiful prayer with a watermarked butterfly imprinted on it.

Just moments before the service started a majestic bald eagle cruised by us along the bluff. Those of us that noticed were speechless. You see, several years earlier when Grandpa Claude was being laid to rest, a bald eagle flew by us along that same bluff, just as his service was about to begin. We all remembered this and looked at each other as if to say, "Did that really just happen?" Each and every one of us felt the connection of an eagle flying by at the start of both Grandma Georgia's and Grandpa Claude's services. Absolutely breathtaking. That would have, in itself, been a story worth sharing.

If you'll allow me to digress, I'd like to step back in time for a moment to highlight why this particular day was so incredibly magical. You see, Grandma's thing with butterflies went well beyond what any of us within our family and friends had ever thought possible.

For many years, whenever she and Grandpa were together, fishing on a lake, camping with us kids, in their travels through the Pacific Northwest and Canada, Monarch Butterflies seemed to be attracted to her. It was like they had some sort of unique connection or fascination with her. I remember a time when she and Grandpa Claude were up in Canada. I called them to check in on how things were going, to see how the fishing was, and to hear of their latest adventures.

Grandma Georgia said to me, "Curtis, you'll never guess what!"

"Well, I'm sure I don't know," I said, "but I'll bet you're going to tell me."

She went on, "Claude and I rented a boat, we were out on this beautiful lake, and we had a visitor."

"A visitor?" I asked.

"Yes," she continued, "as we were fishing, the most beautiful Monarch Butterfly found us, it landed on my hat and stayed there for the longest time."

Every time this happened there was always an element of amazement because this happened so often over the years.

As kids we spent our summers at Grandma & Grandpa's cabin on the deep blue, crystal clear shores of Lake Crescent. It's located in the

Olympic National Park and is one of my favorite places on earth. The two of them would often head out in their boat to enjoy an afternoon cruise or do a little fishing, only to return with yet another story of how a Monarch flew in and landed on the boat or on Grandma's fishing rod, her hat, or shoulder, etc. We always felt a sense of wonder and fascination about it, but as it was common we also considered it to be no big deal. It was her special thing and just another fun fact in the family.

When Grandpa Claude passed away, the butterflies kept coming. By this time Grandma would always claim it was Gramps paying her and the rest of us a visit.

One summer afternoon we were at the lake property enjoying a visit with some friends. As we sat talking around the campfire, we began sharing stories with them about Grandma's encounters with butterflies. God's honest truth, in mid conversation, a Monarch Butterfly flew in and landed on Grandma's arm. Each and every one of us & especially our friends were literally speechless! Again…this too would be story enough.

So, on this particular spring morning, as we gathered for Grandma Georgia's funeral & just after the bald eagle graced us with its presence, the service began. When the pastor eventually brought the service to a close, I turned to my cousins and close family members to say hello and acknowledge them as we had arrived late. Just as I had turned away from my grandmother's casket, my mother wailed, "Oh Dear God!" When I whirled back around, I saw my mother with her hands on her face, my Aunt Gloria on her knees and my Uncle Jim standing there speechless in disbelief. The rest of us were wondering what was going on…

As our family & friends took in the scene, we witnessed an amazing, little miracle on my grandmother's casket. You see, besides the watermarked butterfly in her prayer guide, there was also a beautiful bouquet of flowers with a decorative butterfly on top of her casket. The miracle on that day was that just as the service ended, a Monarch Butterfly landed next to the decorative butterfly among the flowers on her casket. I have told this story many times over the years, and I have yet to tell it without feeling the tears.

After I put these memories to paper, I called my sister and asked her what her own recollection was of that particular day. It was pretty much the same as mine, however she told me that she remembered seeing the butterfly approach and circle us and our cousins as we stood together. It then dropped down and landed on the crafted butterfly among the flowers on Grandma's casket. She said for a brief moment in time she felt like a little girl again.

There is no doubt in our minds that angels were truly among us and our beloved Hoppers that memorable day.

PS: After the service that morning I slowly drove around the entire property in search of perhaps one more butterfly but there were none to be seen.

Curt Ingram is the author of the upcoming book: Exceptional Living with Crohn's and Colitis. He is a former fishing pro and now spends his time as an entrepreneur and public speaker. His theme song is Tim McGraw's: Live like you were dying! He lives & loves life accordingly. Find him at exceptionalnow.blogspot.com

The Three Bears
Polly Johnson

I was packing up my life and preparing to leave my home and everything I knew to bring myself and my child to what I prayed would be a safer place for us.

We had been through the ringer...and my goal was to preserve our life and start over. Starting over was no easy feat, but I knew that despite how weak I was, God was still on my side.

Late in the evening I walked out into my enclosed, forested backyard in Northern California's alpine territory, and as I trustingly stepped off my back porch, I came about twelve feet into the darkness of my property. Hearing what I thought likely to be a raccoon, I turned the dark corner to the side of my barn and came face to face with a roughly 400-pound mama bear.

The wildfires in our area had been extreme and pushed these creatures out of their normal environment and into neighboring properties, and they were desperate to find food. This mama had discovered a brand new thirty-pound bag of dog food outside my door, had ripped it open and was happily grazing there in the darkness until I arrived.

My entire property was fenced and there was no way to simply chase her out. She was also four times my size. She stopped what she was doing, stared at me, and I froze, sensing a presence between us.

I spoke to her calmly, and she watched me for a moment and then turned and moved toward the back end of my property.

There I heard a loud and eerily distinct tearing sound coming from my trees, a sound I had never heard before. Then one smaller and one mid-sized (still larger than me) cub emerged from the 100-foot cedars in my yard...and then there were three.

They had clearly taken up residence at my home, the place we lovingly called "The Funny Farm." On the funny farm, we had three rescue dogs, two rescue cats and three ducks (who had been my son's therapy animals and had been with us the longest, the better part of a decade). Our duckies were fully domesticated; they had no idea that they were ducks and did not know how to fly, they only knew how to be my son's beloved companions, as he had raised them all from just days old ducklings. They would faithfully sit and listen to him perform stand up comedy as a young-un or follow his every move in a waddle line around the yard as they listened intently to him describe their roles in his animated series "The Funny Farm." Lucky, Heimlich, and Mr. Mike (all named after Pixar characters) were as much a part of my child and our life as any family member could be.

On this late night the ducks were still out, huddling fearfully in the corner of the yard not to be seen by the intruders. The bears themselves tore down my wire fencing and left the immediate premises once they recognized a human's presence.

Certain that they were gone, I ushered the duckies into the metal dog kennel we had set up for them just outside my back door for bedtime.

The following evening a friend came by. Still shaken by my mother bear encounter, the friend prayed over my property and boldly sang a sacred Hawaiian prayer chant outside in my yard, under the stars, which was powerful and made me feel at peace with the situation. This friend was a giant Hawaiian man and held a great deal of presence and authority. He reminded me of a warrior angel himself; and this was his particular sacred ritual song for cleansing the energies on the property.

When he was done with his melodic prayer, he looked around and said to me, "There are angels all over this place. They are everywhere. Nothing is going to touch you here." I asked him if I should be worried about the mother bear. He said that there will be forces that will come at us, but none will break through the spiritual barrier and be able to harm us. He told me that I must leave the property as soon as possible, which was the plan. And that there would be an attack, but that he had called angels down all over the property to stand guard and see that we were not harmed. He then unbuttoned his cardigan sweater, placing it over my shoulders and told me to wear that sweater for protection until I get to where I am going. Then he left my home late into the evening. And feeling the comfort of his sweater, and the power of his presence that lingered in it, I kept it on and wore it to bed.

That night I had what felt like a living dream, one of a kind, I had never had before. I felt as though my body were literally "on fire," and I was being held down by the Holy Spirit in my sleep, not allowed to wake.

I could hear the sounds of my ducks calling out in terror, I could hear the screeching and crashing of metal, and I could feel my body burning. And I was fighting to wake up, but I could not. This was not like me at all. I was naturally a very light sleeper and naturally on guard. In my sleep I could feel a presence greater than myself keeping me there in that state.

I realize now I was being held in that place by the Holy Spirit; for had I awakened too soon amidst what was happening at my home, I would have thrown myself into sacrifice impulsively without thinking in an instinctive effort to save our babies.

I finally awoke to an early morning chill, walked outside to the crunchy, frosted grass and the nearly naked trees bearing their arms in silent witness to my horror. Just outside my door, where our beloved pets would greet me with happy quacks every morning from their protective steel dog kennel, was just a mangled mess of metal and remains of those we loved. My entire yard, just the aftermath of lives brutally taken. As I struggled to get ahold of myself and frantically clean up the carcasses that were spread everywhere, which was the most gruesome and heart wrenching experience of my life...I was overwhelmed with guilt and shame for not knowing better, not doing better, not perceiving this risk and being more proactive.

How could I not think that a gigantic bear with two others, would not have the strength to crush a steel cage? How could I not anticipate that they would go after our pets when I had eliminated the dog food and other food sources? And more importantly, how could I have failed these innocent creatures, and more my son?? How could I have been this bad? My mind went everywhere in the sense of my being responsible for this tragedy. And I had plenty of time to think because this was a huge mess. Every time I thought I had it all I would find a foot here or a bill or a wing there. And ~Oh My God~ the pain that was pulsating through my veins...as I remembered the early days of our first Papa Duck Lucky, playing a game with our old lab Happy we liked to call "Happy Go Lucky," where Lucky would chase Happy around the yard and then jump on his back to take a ride.

Lucky lost his mate Ducky to a predator early on, and we thought he was going to die of a broken heart, so we got two babies, Heimlich and Mr. Mike, to keep him company. He was the best Papa Duck and the best, most loyal friend. The three never even thought about flying, I don't even think it occurred to them as an option that they could "fly away" ever...and I promised to protect them, so it was never a thing. They just lived like our dogs. Oh, the horror of it all closing in on me.

As I picked up the mangled metal of what was their home, and pried Lucky's head from the chain link, there before me lied a true miracle.

Completely unscathed in the massacre, and without the shelter of his body, lay before me, Lucky's heart....perfect and beautiful. The last part of him for me to find, as some sort of blessed assurance that he knew he was loved, beyond what any duck could be, and he loved us too....

I remember standing in the kitchen with my son when he woke up, not allowing him outside for most of that day as I cleaned up the yard...weeping with him...the sound of his guttural cry that I couldn't take away...the groanings of his little heart processing this unthinkable loss, not knowing what to do except pray over him in my kitchen and instruct him to do the same, and to write a love letter to his babies.

Nature is cruel. Even a year later I feel terribly responsible and guilty, for not knowing and doing better...and yet I also know that had I been awake and "in the moment," my impulsiveness very well may have gotten me killed. I know that these beloved creatures gave their life for me. I know that they knew they were loved, and they loved us...and that I gave them a very happy and full life. Still, when you are bonded to anything, human or animal, and they are a part of your life, the loss is immense.

I called the County game warden out to discuss how I should remedy the issue. He came to the house and reviewed the video footage from the game cameras I had outside my home and mounted on my barn. We calculated that prior to the kill, the mother bear was pacing outside my back door in what the warden referred to as "a stalking attack mode." She did this for several hours up on my back porch in the middle of the night, before ultimately taking our pets. The warden was convinced that the bear was a danger to me and my son, and that this behavior was characteristic of a predatory hunt. He was surprised that the bear had not come through our back door and into my home; and based on the behavior he said that we were dealing with a bear in what he called a "murder mode." He informed me that my only option was to take out the bear and the cubs (this even against his will, simply due to the present danger); and that they would not assist in a relocation because the mother bear had displayed the intent to endanger humans. In his terms, he indicated what my friend had the night before the incident; that I should leave the property for safety as soon as possible or take the lives of the predators. He was certain that they had made themselves comfortable with me and my home, and there was nothing stopping them from doing further harm or damage to us.

I told Julian that the game warden came out and gave us the option to kill the bears. I did not tell him my heart about that, but rather wanted to see what he would say. He spoke my heart, saying that it was just nature being nature. "That Mama felt desperate and was just doing what any mama would do to take care of her babies...it was just bears being bears," my sweet son said over tears, in the midst of his tragic loss.

So, we collectively decided to leave them alone, allowing them to live in our space. I told the game warden that coming face to face with a bear as I did was a once in a lifetime experience; and something in my spirit made a connection with her. The warden agreed, in his own words telling me that she "felt my protective and healing energy." Nevertheless, my "good vibes" energy making the bears feel safe and comfortable on our property versus elsewhere, was also what put our safety in jeopardy. And in this case, we were now in a situation of "hunt or be hunted."

The game warden warned me of the potential outcome, gave me permission to do what was necessary; and applauded the bravery and heart behind my ultimate decision.

Regardless of what it had cost us, I felt that those three (not so little) bears somehow felt my own protective energy and that I was their safe place. And that's what I want, actually. That is my heart for every living being...to be a safe place for them.

Nature is cruel and unyielding, and though we have to live in it, we don't have to become it. I had the option under the law to take the lives of those who came into our territory and took life from us, but I wouldn't do it because that is never my heart. And sometimes it takes the most gut wrenching of circumstances to actually remind us of the position of our heart: who we are at the core. I did not fail anyone, even if I "think" I did. I was not responsible for what occurred in nature. I was not guilty of harming my precious child or our beloved pets. It just happened. What happens to us does not make us bad. It just is. It can be gruesome and deeply painful, but it is our response to that pain and not the cause of the pain or the act that induces it, which makes us who we are.

Normally in the colder months, I would have set up temporary housing for the duckies in my laundry room, which was right inside my back door, to keep them out of the icy elements and the harsh winter snow. The warden said that had the ducks been inside my back door, the bears would have almost assuredly broken the door down, which was not properly secure, to get to them inside the house. This would have given them free reign in the home.

Given that we were moving, and our furniture and belongings were all packed, my son and I were sleeping on a cot together on the living room floor, laying in front of the wood stove to keep warm. In the event of bears entering our home, he said, given the circumstances and our positioning and lack of a viable escape, the situation for us would very well have turned fatal.

That morning, in my deepest grief, I went to make myself a cup of tea to help calm my nerves. Still shaken at the events of the past twelve hours; my friend's prayers over the property, the words, feelings, even premonitions that he had shared with me just hours before this tragedy still swirling in my mind like a strange and terrible dream.

When I opened the tea bag casing to set the bag in my mug, I noticed the written note attached to the top of the tea bag string.

It read: A blessed presence will protect you from a mischievous intruder.

And so, it was...the giant Hawaiian angel man was right. And I realized, I was still wearing his sweater.

Polly Johnson is a mother, Jesus follower, health and wellness enthusiast, coach, passionate writer and spiritual intuitive, who loves to help people heal and connect to God and their truest being. She credits God for healing her son from Autism and guiding her in that journey. She has a special heart for helping others with this struggle, and for serving families with special needs. Polly can be reached at email: 1divineappointment@gmail.com

Julian's letter to the ducks

Top Photo from right to left- Mr. Mike (female- her name starts with "Mr." because of a personal joke), Heimlich (male) both Black Swedish Ducks
Bottom Photo: Lucky (Chocolate Runner)

Guiding Me Home
Shiran Cohen

There were many moments and periods in my life when I believed I was alone, and had no one to turn to. I used to keep all my secrets to myself and nurture the shame that was growing within me. The experience of life felt painful and dishonest as if I was putting on different masks in front of different people, just enough to fit in but not enough to belong.

One day I stared at my reflection in the mirror, I gazed deep into my eyes and realized that I didn't know who I was anymore. I wondered whose life I'd been living. So I asked loudly almost out of desperation, "Who are you? Who are you? Tell me now who are you? Stop hiding!" I kept staring into my reflection for a while and nothing… I had no answers and no breakthroughs. So I walked away from the mirror.

Several days later I was watching a video of a woman that teaches about consciousness, and something she said sparked the thought *"remember that you are a soul."* It just hit me in the heart. *"Before, during, and after you are 'Shiran.' You are a soul."*

I wanted to understand more, to know why I'm here and whether I was living life as I should. I grew up in a faithful home, and God was always present in my life. At some point I lost faith until I learned and understood the divine system we are all living in. That doesn't mean I know everything, I just realized that everything that feels good in my thoughts, words, emotions, and actions is conducive to my soul's essence.

This process of gaining a deeper understanding of how to know when something is in alignment with my journey on this earth, restored my faith in God. In essence, I gained clarity, identity and confidence. I gained faith that I have the wisdom to navigate my journey in this life with God as my constant source of wisdom. Ever since then my faith has been whole.

The conversations I now have with God are intimate and honest. I notice the many "coincidences" in my life. I have so many examples of situations when I can sense how someone I love and have a deep connection with is feeling. It is not a physical feeling but an emotional one.

I could be asking God a question and just passing by the TV at the right moment to see the answer. I can drive in my car, telling God what is on my heart and suddenly the next song on the radio seems like God is speaking back to me through the lyrics. It fills my heart with comfort and joy to know that such a big God cares about me enough to communicate with me in the most subtle of ways. Because of this I know that I am loved.

It's been a long time since I allowed faith back into my life and I'm so happy I have it because now even when I feel like I'm alone I know immediately that I'm not.

About three months ago I was driving to a store to pick up tiles. I arrived there and one store employee loaded the needed tiles. Everything was great. I started to drive back home, and within a minute everything had changed, and I realized that I could easily find myself in a very dangerous situation.

There is something you need to know. I live in Israel which is a beautiful and unique country but even in the holy land we have problems like hate and violence, terrorism, and ego. About eighteen months ago there was chaos in Israel, missiles were flying and in addition to a war against terrorist organizations, there was also an inner war between Muslims and Jews. People were brutally attacked, lynched, injured, and even killed. The attackers weren't outsiders but neighbors, work colleagues, and strangers on the street.

Here I was - a Jewish woman driving by myself in a Muslim Arab village. This was the same village that participated in the chaos and violence against Jewish people the year prior. I was minutes away from accidentally taking the wrong turn and driving directly to the West Bank. To make matters worse I was not familiar with the area.

Realizing that I needed to take all necessary precautions to keep myself out of harm's way, I set the GPS on my smartphone but after a minute it died. I immediately tried to charge it, but the charger wasn't working.

Next, I tried the car GPS but that didn't work.

I didn't know how to find the road back home, and all my technology was not working, I couldn't call anyone and if I asked someone outside for directions - they would know I'm Jewish from my accent and I might be at risk.

"What am I supposed to do now?" I thought to myself, *"I'm alone. No, Shiran, that's a lie! You know that God is always with you. Ask God."*

And so I did…

"God, you've placed me here to be your partner in this life journey, feel my heart and show me a safe way home." I said this sentence out loud in my car and within thirty seconds I saw a roundabout with bushes and low trees, then I saw something blue hiding in the bushes. As I drove closer, I saw that it was a small sign about five inches, shaped as an arrow with the words "Road 6" on it. My heart immediately replaced any fear with faith.

I prayed, "God you are with me, you are answering me - lead me home."

At this point I still had a fifteen-minute drive to "Road 6," and many more turns until I would arrive home. I continued driving and held in my heart "show me the way home."

As I was driving, I saw another small sign, then another after a few minutes of "guessing" and being led by a "feeling" to the correct turns.

Suddenly I felt my heart turn "heavy" and something inside told me to stop and turn around. That hunch got stronger and more intense, so I turned around and after three minutes - I returned to a place I had already been. That is when I noticed that I had missed a sign and took a wrong turn before! The sign was so poorly located behind a statue that I completely overlooked it.

There was probably about five more minutes until I would arrive at "Road 6." I was driving and there were no signs. I kept driving and knew I was getting closer but didn't know where to turn.

I arrived at a place where there were five roads to choose from… and no signs. Suddenly, I saw a truck passing with the name of a factory located in a city in the North of Israel. I was headed North too! I decided to follow the truck and within ninety seconds, I found "Road 6." From there I knew my way home.

"Thank you, God," I whispered, "for keeping me safe and guiding me back home."

As I said before, this is just one of many times when God has shown Himself to be a faithful friend and protector. The more experiences I have with Him the more I trust Him.

What I have learned in my spiritual journey is this:

In every moment, I have the choice to listen to my insecurities and pride or simply remember that I'm a soul on a journey. Everyone has this choice. Therefore there is no reason to be angry, stressed, sad, and holding in my heart unpleasant emotions because, in my essence, there is kindness, love, forgiveness, and joy so when I behave that way towards myself and others it is simply who I am. Every time I'm choosing faith I feel blessed, I feel at home.

Shiran Cohen is an international bestselling author and coach. If you would like more guidance in the process, she created a journal with a process you can use as a roadmap in your journey. It's called, EXPLORE Your CONSCIOUSNESS: MIND & SOUL Journal and can be found wherever books are sold. To reach Shiran, email: shiran.public@gmail.com.

Angel Numbers
Lynisha Senegal

Have you ever noticed yourself stumbling upon repeating number sequences like 111, 555 or 777? Maybe you wake up from a nap at 2:22, then you buy a cup of coffee for $2.22, then you watch a movie that is two hours and twenty-two minutes long. It might not be a coincidence. It's as if each number has a vibrational energy and is a sign to continue along the path you are on. Usually, with 222 - it means change is coming. It could also speak to relationships and heart connections.

Repeating numbers serve as an amplification of energy. The more a number shows up around a person, the stronger the vibrational energy is behind it. This can influence a person's life or help them make a difficult decision. It means the full power of that energy is present.

I believe God speaks to us in synchronistic ways. I am the type of person who sees angel numbers everywhere. Numbers like 111, 222, 333 and so on. Whenever I see 555, it reminds me of God's grace, even if I am out of sync with my actions. When I see 111, to me it means I am aligned in order with God. It's a powerful manifestation and visualization of goals and dreams.

When I am praying for something and I see 777, it means it's final and approved. It gives me the faith to feel spiritually aligned. The number 777 is basically God and the Universe telling you to relax and let go of fears for the future. It helps me embrace the present and trust that I am being guided. The Universe always has a way of auto-correcting and I know the power of Who walks next to me at all times. So, why should I have fear?

I recently had some health issues and the doctors found a big knot in my throat. They ran some tests and were not sure if it was cancer or not. I'm a holistic person and don't like doing surgery or major medical treatments if they are not necessary. So I decided to wait on my own healing. After a year and a half, the knot was still there. The doctors insisted that we do surgery.

Before I went to surgery, I was questioning the doctors and wanted to wait for my own healing. I was prepared to cancel the surgery, then I saw the number 111 as it popped up on my phone. I saw that as confirmation that God wanted me to have the surgery, so I had it done. They were able to fully remove the knot.

As it turns out, the knot was thyroid cancer and I had been carrying it for a long time. They said it was very rare and should have spread to my blood, but because of how hard the mass was, it actually prevented the cancer from spreading.

I can now see that doctors are an extension of God's hands. I also didn't have to do any chemotherapy, radiation or take any type of cancer medication. When we pray, we are expecting to be healed and sometimes we can't do it on our own. I continue to see angel numbers daily and love feeling that connection with God that I am on the right path in my life and business.

Lynisha Senegal created a mission for minority business owners to create generational wealth through pathways of ownership. She is grateful to own a 33,000 square foot commercial property to help with this mission. For more information, visit: www.visionviewca.com or email: hopedailyls@gmail.com.

Angels Among Us

CONCLUSION

We hope these stories have inspired you to be open to your own angel experiences.

For additional resources from the book, or information on sharing your own story in one of our books, please visit our website:

www.MyDefiningMoments.com

Angels Among Us

About Defining Moments Press

Built for aspiring authors who are looking to share transformative ideas with others throughout the world, Defining Moments Press offers life coaches, healers, business professionals, and other non-fiction or self-help authors a comprehensive solution to getting their books published without breaking the bank or taking years.

Defining Moments Press prides itself on bringing readers and authors together to find tools and solutions.

As an alternative to self-publishing or signing with a major publishing house, we offer full profits to our authors, low-priced author copies, and simple contract terms.

Most authors get stuck trying to navigate the technical end of publishing. The comprehensive publishing services offered by Defining Moments Press mean that your book will be designed by an experienced graphic artist, available in printed, hard copy format, and coded for all eBook readers, including the Kindle, iPad, Nook, and more.

We handle all of the technical aspects of your book creation so you can spend more time focusing on your business that makes a difference for other people.

Defining Moments Press founder, publisher, and #1 bestselling author Melanie Warner has over twenty years of experience as a writer, publisher, master life coach, and accomplished entrepreneur.

You can learn more about Warner's innovative approach to self-publishing or take advantage of free trainings and education at: MyDefiningMoments.com.

Angels Among Us

Defining Moments Book Publishing

If you're like many authors, you have wanted to write a book for a long time, maybe you have even started a book...but somehow, as hard as you have tried to make your book a priority, other things keep getting in the way.

Some authors have fears about their ability to write or whether or not anyone will value what they write or buy their book. For others, the challenge is making the time to write their book or having accountability to finish it.

It's not just finding the time and confidence to write that is an obstacle. Most authors get overwhelmed with the logistics of finding an editor, finding a support team, hiring an experienced designer, and figuring out all the technicalities of writing, publishing, marketing, and launching a book. Others have actually written a book and might have even published it but did not find a way to make it profitable.

For more information on how to participate in our next Defining Moments Author Training program, visit: www.MyDefiningMoments.com Or you can email melanie@MyDefiningMoments.com.

Angels Among Us

OTHER BOOKS BY DEFINING MOMENTS PRESS

Bible Study Lessons: Weekly Plans for Church Leaders Volume 1, 2 & 3 - John Warner

Defining Moments: Coping With the Loss of a Child - Melanie Warner

Defining Moments SOS: Stories of Survival - Melanie Warner and Amber Torres

Defining Moments: Angels Among Us - Melanie Warner and Amber Torres

Write your Bestselling Book in 8 Weeks or Less and Make a Profit - Even if No One Has Ever Heard of You - Melanie Warner

Become Brilliant: Roadmap From Fear to Courage – Shiran Cohen

Unspoken: Body Language and Human Behavior For Business - Shiran Cohen

Rise, Fight, Love, Repeat: Ignite Your Morning Fire - Jeff Wickersham

Life Mapping: Decoding the Blueprint of Your Soul - Karen Loenser

Ravens and Rainbows: A Mother-Daughter Story of Grit, Courage and Love After Death – L. Grey and Vanessa Lynn

Pivot You! 6 Powerful Steps to Thriving During Uncertain Times – Suzanne R. Sibilla

A Workforce Inspired: Tools to Manage Negativity and Support a Toxic-Free Workplace – Dolores Neira

Journey of 1000 Miles: A Musher and His Huskies' Journey on the Century-Old Klondike Trails - Hank DeBruin and Tanya McCready

*7 Unstoppable Starting Powers: Powerful Strategies For Unparalleled Results From Your First Year as a New Leade*r – Olusegun Eleboda

Bouncing Back From Divorce With Vitality & Purpose: A Strategy For Dads – Nigel J Smart, PHD

Focus on Jesus and Not the Storm: God's Non-negotiables to Christians in America - Keith Kelley

Stepping Out, Moving Forward: Songs and Devotions - Jacqueline O'Neil Kelley

Time Out For Time In: How Reconnecting With Yourself Can Help You Bond With Your Child in a Busy Word - Jerry Le

The Sacred Art of Off Mat Yoga: Whisper of Wisdom Forever – Shakti Barnhill

The Beauty of Change: The Fun Way For Women to Turn Pain Into Power & Purpose – Jean Amor Ramoran

From No Time to Free Time: 6 Steps to Work/Life Balance For Business Owners - Christoph Nauer

Self-Healing For Sexual Abuse Survivors: Tired of Just Surviving, Time to Thrive - Nickie V. Smith

Frog on a Lily Pad - Michael Lehre

How to Effectively Supercharge Your Career as a CEO - Giorgio Pasqualin

Rising From Unsustainable: Replacing Automobiles and Rockets - J.P. Sweeney

Food - Life's Gift for Healing: Simple, Delicious & Life Saving Whole Food Plant Based Solutions - Angel and Terry Grier

Harmonize All of You With All: The Leap Ahead in Self-Development - Artie Vipperla

Powerless to Powerful: How to Stop Living in Fear and Start Living Your Life - Kat Spencer

Living with Dirty Glasses: How to Clean thos Dirty Glasses and Gain a Clearer Perspective Of Your Life - Leah Spelt Ligia

The Road Back to You: Finding Your Way After Losing a Child to Suicide - Trish Simonson

Gavin Gone: Turning Pain into Purpose to Create a Legacy - Rita Gladding

The Health Nexus: TMJ, Sleep Apnea, and Facial Development, Causations and Treatment - Robert Perkins DDS

Samantha Jean's Rainbow Dream: A Young Foster Girl's Adventure into the Colorful World of Fruits & Vegetables - AJ Autieri - Luciano

Please Excuse My Brave: Overcoming Fear and Living Out Your Purpose - Anisa L. Wesley

Unstoppable: A Parent's Survival Guide for Special Education Services with an IEP or 504 Plan - Raja Marhaba

Made in the USA
Las Vegas, NV
17 December 2022

63106710R00056